EMAIL MARKETING

How to Increase Your E-mail Marketing Profits

(Discover How to Grow Your Business With the Power of Email)

Sherry Hasting

Published By Sherry Hasting

Sherry Hasting

All Rights Reserved

Email Marketing: How to Increase Your E-mail Marketing Profits (Discover How to Grow Your Business With the Power of Email)

ISBN 978-1-77485-436-5

All rights reserved. No part of this guide may be reproduced in any form without permission in writing from the publisher except in the case of brief quotations embodied in critical articles or reviews.

Legal & Disclaimer

The information contained in this book is not designed to replace or take the place of any form of medicine or professional medical advice. The information in this book has been provided for educational and entertainment purposes only.

The information contained in this book has been compiled from sources deemed reliable, and it is accurate to the best of the Author's knowledge; however, the Author cannot guarantee its accuracy and validity and cannot be held liable for any errors or omissions. Changes are periodically made to this book. You must consult your doctor or get professional medical advice before using any of the suggested remedies, techniques, or information in this book.

Upon using the information contained in this book, you agree to hold harmless the Author from and against any damages, costs, and expenses, including any legal fees potentially resulting from the application of any of the information provided by this guide. This disclaimer applies to any damages or injury caused by the use and application, whether directly or indirectly, of any advice or information presented, whether for breach of contract, tort, negligence, personal injury, criminal intent, or under any other cause of action.

You agree to accept all risks of using the information presented inside this book. You need to consult a professional medical practitioner in order to ensure you are both able and healthy enough to participate in this program.

TABLE OF CONTENTS

INTRODUCTION 1

CHAPTER 1: WHAT IS EMAIL MARKETING? 3

CHAPTER 2: DIFFERENT TYPES OF MARKETING E-MAIL 6

CHAPTER 3: DIFFERENT KINDS OF MESSAGES 26

CHAPTER 4: MAKING A HUGE EMAIL LIST 44

CHAPTER 5: HOW TO OPTIMIZE YOUR MARKETING VIA EMAIL 92

CHAPTER 6: HOW TO KEEP MESSAGES OUT OF THE SPAM FOLDER 123

CHAPTER 7: HOW TO CREATE RELEVANT MESSAGING USING EFFECTIVE SUBJECT LINES AND SMART DESIGNS 167

CONCLUSION 183

Introduction

This book provides the most effective steps and strategies for how to create an email marketing list which expands the customer base of your company...

Are you interested in the use of e-mail marketing? You may have thought that e-mail marketing could be effective in promoting your small business, but you're no idea how this strategy is actually working.

The best part is that marketing via e-mail aren't very difficult and can be utilized by almost anyone.

Every business owner should be incorporating them into their marketing plans.

Marketing via email is among the best return on advertising that money can purchase. According to studies conducted by various marketing firms over the last five years, email marketing strategies can yield approximately an income of $45 per dollar spent.

This is a very cost-effective way of marketing!

This approach to advertising has been used by 100s of corporations all over the world. If your business isn't a part of this movement, you could be missing out on clients, revenue as well as brand awareness. Just like everything within business, you have to start somewhere. This is the best time to begin your company's email marketing campaign. This book will allow you to start quickly and effortlessly.

Thank you thank you for downloading the book. I hope that you will enjoy it!

Chapter 1: What Is Email Marketing?

Marketing via email isn't an incredibly difficult matter. It is generally a matter of including the use of emails in your small business's marketing plan.

It's the same thing in sending out mailings, coupons and newsletters books by postal mail, however it's delivered through email. Most of your clients utilize email as a method of communication. This means that you'll likely be getting contact with them daily!

There are many methods to use the e-mail marketing method to advertise your business and your products and services to clients. It is important to use the power of e-mail marketing to reach prospective clients via their own private computers, or to begin employing these strategies to promote your business in public places. Here are some great examples of how to market your business via e-mail:

Direct marketing emails

E-mails sent to new customers

E-mails sent to clients who are already customers

Offers to reward customers
Marketing and email ads.

E-mail marketing strategies are appreciated by small businesses due to a variety of reasons. For one, it allows you to connect with hundreds or thousands of people daily. That means your latest products, services, and marketing offers could be able to reach potential customers several times per day, in just only a few seconds. E-mail marketing allows you to definitely reach out and connect to your customers easily and efficiently.

E-mail marketing strategies can be extremely cost effective. The process of sending out an e-mail can be inexpensive, particularly as compared to other small-scale business marketing strategies like direct mail and SEO strategies.

Furthermore, marketing via email offer a distinct advantage over many other forms of marketing for small businesses due to the fact that they allow you to direct contact with potential customers. It is true that online users can discover everything they want to know about your business through your site however they have to start taking the necessary actions to get there. When you use e-mail marketing, you're trying to connect with your customers without having to do anything at all.

Additionally, email marketing techniques have proven to be a successful method for smaller companies to market themselves, provided that the methods are used correctly. This means you can begin the whole process of creating an email marketing strategy for your smaller company with the confidence that if you implement the right thing, you'll get positive results! This is the reason why email marketing techniques are extremely popular with many small and local businesses.

Chapter 2: Different Types Of Marketing E-Mail

There are three general kinds of marketing strategies via email that you can employ.

Each one of them can help you locate and keep more customers.

The first kind of marketing via email is known as direct e-mail which is just what it's called. This particular method is the practice of sending targeted marketing messages as well with promotions to your client's email address. These messages could be announcements of special deals such as great deals, sales or other offers.

They could be employed to let people know regarding any new service your business offers or about new areas it is able to currently serve. They will typically include a "call to action" in them, which prompts customers to take a specific action in order to get a discount offer. The 'call to action could ask users to sign up to receive a service, go to the website of your company, or call.

Direct e-mails basically tell your customers about what's going on within your business, and all they need to do is open the email.

The other type of email marketing is actually known as retention emailing. Retention emails are created not just to inform your clients about your company's offerings and services, but also to build a lasting connection with them. Retention emails offer more than just promotional messages and ads; they contain information that can be valuable for the person reading.

These kinds of emails contain information that is designed to be informative, entertaining and interactive with the recipient in order to ensure that they have some kind of interaction with your fantastic small-scale company.

The most commonly used method of e-mails for retention that are used in e-mail marketing strategies is newsletters.

The third tactic for marketing via e-mail is straight-up email advertising but you'll use e-mail content that was developed by another company. This involves attaching your company's message to an e-mail or newsletter produced by another business. You may have received an e-mail in the past. an other business's advertisement is placed on the bottom, top or even the sides of the email.

This is also an extremely effective method to make use of e-mail marketing in order to increase your small business's marketing impact.

Benefits of Email Benefits Of Email Business

Email marketing campaigns can assist small businesses build loyalty, understanding and trust with customers. It is a great way to keep and retain your company's existing customers as well as to help to attract new ones simultaneously.

Here are some ways in which an appropriately planned E-mail marketing campaign can help your small-scale business:

1. E-mail marketing campaigns can be extremely economical.

Direct marketing strategies require an adequate amount of money in order to be successful mostly due to the fact that they are creating real material, such as an advertisement printed on paper or a newsletter. You will then end up spending more money to mail this content that is authentic to your clients via post.

Marketing via email still uses electronic content, which is much cheaper to develop, as well as distributes it to your customers electronically. The process of sending out content electronically is less costly than sending it to the real world. This means that you are able to reach thousands or hundreds of potential customers for less than the cost that are associated with direct marketing.

2. Marketing via email is targeted.

You can target specific clients with email marketing. This means that you are able to concentrate on communicating with those who will be interested in receiving your messages and spend time and money trying to reach out to people who do not wish to hear from you. Also, this saves your marketing department cash and time.

3. Marketing via email allows you to monitor information.

Since marketing via e-mail is conducted electronically, it is extremely easy to monitor your data and assess whether your strategy is effective. For instance, it's easy to determine the number of people who actually read your email, the number of people who decided to opt out of your emails, who forwards your advertisements to another person and also who marked your e-mails as spam. All of this data can be gathered quickly and easily from all of your potential customers.

This system of data tracking helps marketers to determine the methods of marketing via email are producing positive results and which are just wasting time and energy. When you are able to comprehend the value of this information, you will be capable of altering your strategies for advertising and marketing to ensure they're more effective.

4. Marketing via email could be automated.

Once you've got an idea of the types of content you would like to share with your customers through your e-mail marketing strategy, it's simple to automatize the process. This means that you'll be able schedule e-mails and newsletters a few weeks or even months ahead and enable you to design the content you desire. You can also create an automated delivery system that will reduce time, time-consuming and cash.

5. Marketing via email is super rapid!

A single of the best advantages of an email marketing strategy is that it operates quickly, and really quick. It's not necessary to wait for days or even weeks to see the outcomes of your marketing campaign via emailResults can be seen within seconds! Your company's emails will immediately be sent to your customers and give up-to-date information as well as content. It is also possible to observe the outcomes of this method of marketing almost immediately. Marketing strategies via email aid small businesses in keeping up-to-date with their clients and function in real-time.

6. Marketing via email can definitely improve the amount of money you earn.

Marketing via email can not only help techniques help you grow its sales and earn more revenues, but these strategies can be done with ease and in a tested and quantifiable method. This type of marketing could bring in sales through different channels. Choose the appropriate email marketing strategy to avoid the detested'spam label, and your business will experience an increase in the income. In the end, the more customers you are able to attract, the higher revenues and sales you'll get!

How to run an email Marketing Campaign

It's obvious why your small-sized business should use the power of e-mail to grow the number of customers, create brand recognition and boost revenue.

There are acceptable and undesirable methods of using this method of marketing. It is crucial that you know the best methods to implement an email marketing strategy so that you don't alienate your clients and getting branded as a spammer.

There are three fundamentals that you need to master before you can anticipate your email marketing campaign to start showing results.

These three essentials include making an inventory of the people who would like to hear your company's message, composing your message in a way that does not come across as spam and establishing the system to deliver the messages to your viewers' inbox.

After you've completed these three basic steps, you are able to explore a variety of more elaborate and advanced strategies to increase your performance.

In the realm of e-mail marketing, there's always the possibility of improvement.

Getting Started

In order to begin the process of developing an effective email marketing strategy for your small business , all you need to do is agree to do it.

Most business owners believe that the notion that they need to be a "marketing expert' to effectively implement an email marketing strategy is the biggest obstacle.

E-mail marketing is much simpler than it appears- as long as you understand the fundamentals right.

Once your company has committed to developing an e-mail marketing plan, then the next thing to do is making your names part of your email list that you send out.

Making an e-mailing list

This is the core for your strategy to market.

You'll need the names of your customers and email addresses to start with, so you can begin sending your marketing emails out to the world. It is likely that your company has a database of past and present clients.

First step gathering all your contact information and names in one place that is easily identifiable. The best method to arrange and categorize your email names is to make use of the database. It doesn't require an academic degree in computer science to utilize a database- you can make use of the Microsoft Excel Spreadsheet or Mac's Mactracker or any other software you're able to operate.

(Look at some tutorials for databases on YouTube to get some easy tips for those who aren't familiar with the use of the database.)

The management of all your addresses with databases makes it simple to view the e-mail addresses that you already have and to add them to your list as time goes by and your business grows.

Start with your company's Rolodex and make the list of past customers, prospective and current customers. You can later purchase or lease names and email addresses to increase your reach in marketing However, you should start by consolidating your current and old customer lists.

Next step would be to find the email addresses of these customers.

If you do not have these addresses, Here are a few ways to obtain the addresses:

Sign-up Sheets

Create an e-mail signup form for customers to supply your email addresses. An effective way to accomplish this is to provide an e-mail signup form on your storefront as well as on your website. Give the person something in exchange in exchange for their email.

For instance:

It could be: "Sign up here to receive a newsletter for free and amazing promotional offers!" Make sure this is a form that has enough space for users to write down their lengthy email addresses and begin with their names and e-mail addresses. If you request excessive information right from the beginning, you could discourage users from signing for the newsletter.

Privacy Beserches

Privacy is very important to consumers and without a solid privacy statement , you're likely to not receive lots of E-mail addresses.

In order to conduct an e-mail marketing campaign you must have the consent of the individuals you plan to send emails to. Sending unwelcome e-mails to someone without their consent is referred to as SPAM. Spam filters in the majority of mail inboxes prevent recipients from receiving your unwelcome emails, and everyone hates spam. If you want to ensure that people be loyal to your company's name and be able to receive your e-mails do not ever, ever send spam!

Spam mail can cause the loss of your customer list, it could result in the loss of your email accounts as well as hosting services for your website.

The consequences of being a spammer could be extremely severe. This means you need to obtain the consent of the owner prior to sending out commercial or marketing e-mails to them.

E-mail marketing campaigns can only be effective when they are founded on consent.

There are a variety of ways to get the consent of a client. It is possible to add an option on your signup form or on your online purchase page that states: "Yes, I would prefer to receive promotional emails".

If they tick the "Yes" box, then they have given your company permission to send them promotional emails. Also, you should create a clear privacy policy, to ensure that your customers can be confident that you're not doing anything illegal or unlawful using their email address.

This privacy statement needs to be made clear for your clients. It should be displayed on your website, at your location, and on everything that requests an e-mail address from a customer. If you're looking for more information about the privacy of e-mails, browse online for resources like www.privacy.org.

Designing Your Campaign

Once there is a record of your customers' names and have taken the necessary steps to obtain their email addresses as well as permission to send messages to them You are now able to create your email marketing campaign.

Remember that the aim of email marketing is to offer something valuable to the recipient so that you can earn their trust, loyalty and convince them to purchase your product or services.

This means you don't wish to overburden your customers with information because this can make them unsubscribe from your newsletter. It is also important not to provide too little information or your customers might forget about your business. An effective e-mail marketing strategy will require you to strike the right proper balance between sending too much information as well as not having enough.

Quality of the content marketing should also be top-quality.

The best methods of ensuring that your clients are always happy receiving your emails is to give them an assortment of various types of content that are delivered at different times. One method of determining this is to consider your own perspective and the way you look at your own email inbox. Consider asking yourself the kinds and types of content you enjoy to read, as well as what types of content or cause you to be annoyed.

Here are a variety of forms and kinds of content your business could offer to its customers. What kinds of content will best match your specific customers?

* News and information

* Editorial content
* Fun content, like anecdotes, jokes and stories.
* Urgent product/service updates
* Price fluctuations
* Recall the information
* Customer notifications about warranties contracts, accounts or warranties.
* Promotional deals
* Order confirmations
* Shipping confirmations
* Up-selling message
* Personal messages like birthday wishes

The objective is to provide email content that is beneficial for the reader, which encourages readers to take actions and will keep them loyal to your business.

Consider what you'd like a business to send you to aid you. Consider informative and useful information, perhaps as an email that provides readers with something they want at no cost. Consider what kinds of deals and offers could encourage you to make the effort to go to their site or shop.

Offer exclusive deals and discounts to loyal customers. Reward them for coming back and repeatedly. Find potential customers and give them the reason to be loyal customers.

If you've got an idea of the way you would like your email marketing campaign be, you can start making each e-mail.

Sending out e-mails to promote your marketing campaign

Spend the time to design excellent marketing emails for your campaign.

This is crucial in the beginning stages, when the viewers must decide whether or not your business email messages are interesting enough to be read.

Here are some suggestions to make your marketing emails worth taking the time to read:

Create a brand new email address that you can use to send outgoing messages. This is a means of using an email address that's not already in the address book of your customer. It should appear professional and doesn't look like an automated e-mail address with lots of numbers and letters.

Make sure to pay attention to the words you use on your subject line. The subject line of your email is crucial as it determines if the recipient will open the email or erase the message. Do not be overly aggressive or exaggerated in the subject line. A lot of promotional words and exclamation points or capitalization in your subject line could cause your email to be classified as spam. Be particularly cautious when you phrase "free".

Make sure that the contents of your marketing emails concise and straight to the point. If your content is lengthy or wordy, chances are that your recipients will not read the message. Create a compelling opening sentence to keep them engaged and make sure you offer readers something that is valuable. Make sure that your message gets straight to the point. The person reading your message will just give you only a couple of seconds So make sure that the content you write is valuable. Include a promo, article about news or an deal. Add hyperlinks to your site and an incentive for the visitor to click this link.

Make sure to use a different email address for customers who are currently on your list. Give your regular customers a special treatmentand let them know that they are appreciated and valued as clients. They will be returning to return. Create a special email for potential customers as well as customers you may have lost as well. Your e-mails should look more personal.

Try out your different email messages before you send them to your clients by sending them out to your coworkers, friends and even to yourself. This will allow you to ensure that your e-mails appear correct and aren't being classified as spam by your inboxes.

• Include a disclaimer in the top of emails which informs the recipient of why they received the email. It should read similar to this: "You are receiving this email because you have subscribed to our service with this email address. If you didn't subscribe to this service, or would prefer to be removed of our services, select the unsubscribe button found at the end of the page".

This is something you should do to comply with this law. Controlling the Assault of Non-Solicited Pornography and Marketing Act of 2003 (CAN-SPAM Act) The act was developed to stop the practice of spamming.

To comply to this law, you must provide the address for your business in the marketing emails you send out.

Here are some additional points to consider to ensure that you are in compliance to the CAN-SPAM Act

Be sure to identify your company and your routing details from the header data. Avoid using incorrect "To" or "From" headers.

Be sure to identify the message you send as being an advertisement. You are able to decide the method you prefer to use for this, but be sure that your email is clear as being an advertisement.

Be sure that your company adheres to its opt-out process. If a customer requests to opt-out of your e-mail marketing service, ensure you remove them from the mailing list. You must eliminate any opt-out clients within 10 calendar days from the date they received the email and your opt-out program must be operational until at minimum 30 calendar days following the email was sent.

Your company is responsible for adhering to CAN-SPAM Act, regardless of whether it contracts out its marketing via e-mail or contracts with a third party to handle it. Make sure any assistance you receive from outside adheres to these rules as well.

* A person may be held responsible for violation of this law and any e-mail that is not properly handled could lead to penalties of up to $16,000.

It is crucial to ensure that your company's e-mail marketing strategy is in line with the law known as the CAN-SPAM Act. For a better understanding of whether your methods are legal, it is recommended that you read the restrictions of the law at the bureau of consumer protection's Business Center. Their website can be found at: http://business.ftc.gov.

Chapter 3: Different Kinds Of Messages

Broadcast Messages and Pre-Loaded Follow-Up messages

There are two kinds of e-mails used in a marketing campaign. These are broadcast messages as well as pre-loaded messages.

Broadcast messages are single-time messages that will be sent out to all of your customers simultaneously. They contain the most recent news and details about your business and are time-sensitive in their nature. They may also include products recommendations, latest deals and promotions, as well as new details about a new product's launch. A bi-weekly or weekly newsletter is an excellent example of broadcast messages.

Pre-loaded messages are commonly utilized in conjunction with an autoresponder system. In this case, written messages are sent automatically to clients at regular intervals. These intervals could be as frequent as each day, every each week, or many times throughout the month. It is important to figure out the amount that will keep your customers entertained but not overloaded.

Certain marketers using e-mails send very brief and obscure messages several times throughout the each day. They usually include an intriguing or mysterious message which entices readers to keep reading. The advantage in preloaded emails is they're prepared with lots of content and are ready for use.

It is essential to prepare plenty of pre-loaded material that can be utilized in your auto responder software, generally more than a months worth.

The content must also be informative, interesting and short in length. The pre-loaded messages shouldn't contain any information that is time-sensitive as well, which means that they are able to be distributed at any moment.

Each of the products, services , and promotions that you provide in your pre-loaded messages should remain available when you announce launch. Pre-loaded messages typically start with an autoresponder, that is followed by numerous follow-up messages.

A good e-mail marketing program makes use of both kinds of messages.

Pre-loaded autoresponder emails work well using time-sensitive broadcast messages to keep your customers up-to-date to what's happening in your company.

For instance:

Your clients could get an autoresponder pre-loaded every couple of days or so. They could also receive an up-to date newsletter twice a week. If they only received autoresponder messages , they will not have the most current information and could become bored of your emails.

If they only receive your broadcast messages only once every two weeks, they may forget about your business over time. The sending of pre-loaded autoresponder messages as well as broadcast emails will be able to cover your needs.

Sending out your E-mails

After you've created the various marketing emails for your clients, it is now time to send your messages out. This is the reason you have made a database of e-mail addresses.

The majority of marketing e-mails are sent out for a period of around three days prior to being usually read and then deleted. You may send your emails out at any time, however studies have proven that sending them out on more productive days during the week, such as Tuesdays and Mondays are the best especially when you're sending emails to businesses. For mailings on weekends to private residences, you may be able to send them on Sundays. The time of day will guarantee that your email will be received and read.

Processing requests to opt out

It is vitally important to promptly address any requests to opt-out from your customers.

The more you are able to comply with your client's requests, the more satisfied they'll be. Even those who not receive your emails still be interested in purchasing your products, therefore it's important to give them the best treatment.

The best method for this is to take every opt-out request from every channel before you address these requests. The opt-out requests could be made to your business via mail, telephone, or even in person.

Make the effort every week or once to check your email contacts list with customers who have chosen to opt-out. This will ensure sure that these clients not receive your marketing email messages.

Bounced messages

When your email marketing campaign progresses, you may start to receive bounced messages. These are emails that are returned to your inbox with the status "undeliverable".

Make sure you collect all of your bounced emails every several days or so and then update your database. This will ensure that you don't make a mistake by sending out emails that will be returned to you.

Here are a few ways to attempt to find the correct email address to send bounced emails:

Re-send bounced messages within about one month. If the message was rejected because the inbox of the recipient was full, they may not receive the message again.

If the client has a contact number, you might want to contact them to inform them that the newsletter or e-mail they requested is not going to be sent to them. (Don't make more than one call as your customers could be on a list of no-callers.)
If you own the address of your customer's postal, you may want to send them a postcard to request an alternative email address. Include a returnable postcard, or a link to your site where they can modify their e-mail address.

Follow-up e-mails

It is crucial to monitor your e-mail clients, both for bounced or unreceived email messages. You may choose to follow up your e mails with additional e-mails via phone calls or by snail mail.

Most of the time , you will send follow-up emails in your autoresponder software, which means that your clients receive automated emails that keep them engaged. The more occasions a person is aware of your advertisements more likely they will keep it in mind.

Use phrases like "last opportunity", "just a couple of days remaining" and "offer expires in a few days" in your follow-up emails. Be aware that you are looking at the subtle harmony of numerous messages to keep your client engaged but not in a way that they could become angry with your company.

How to define your results

After a certain period of time, you will begin to understand the results of your marketing e-mails. You'll have a list of the e-mails that your business has sent out, as well as a list of how many emails were read, deleted and sent out. You'll know the number of customers who have requested to unsubscribe from your emails and how many of them have taken benefit of your promotions.

You might want to send an e-mail specifically to specific clients to inquire whether they enjoyed receiving your emails , and what you can do to improve the performance of your e-mails. The key is to be flexible in your marketing e-mails.

If you find that a certain strategy doesn't work, then change the method you employ. Always keep an eye out for more email addresses and more prospective customers. Test new ideas. Learn from your successes and blunders.

Tools for Marketing Automation that Automated E-Mail

Controlling your marketing e-mail mailing groups and transmitting a plethora of pre-loaded as well as broadcast messages per week is a challenge. This is exactly why you'll discover automated e-mail marketing tools and AEMTs.

These programs simplify the procedure of creating letters that schedule the delivery mail, managing your email address list, and managing opt-outs.

In essence the simplest terms, an AEMT will make the whole email marketing process much simpler to manage.

There are numerous automated programs that are available for purchase on the internet and a few are available for no cost. Simply a Google search can help you locate these software. The majority of small-sized businesses choose to choose one of the three major AEMTs on the market.

The three main AMTs that are the 3 most important include MailChimp, AWeber and Constant Contact.

The three automated tools provide templates for messages as well as automated mail delivery and interfaces that permit users to customize their personal e-mail marketing plan. They have a wide range of features, meaning you'll need to know how to use their features and tools. Tutorials will make learning significantly easier.

Here's a quick overview of the three most important AEMTs.

MailChimp is completely free to start using, making it a preferred option for those who are new to the world of marketing via email. So long as your email address list contains less than 2000 users and you are sending out less than 12,000 emails every month, you are able to make use of MailChimp's service for no cost.

Over that amount, there is an additional fee per month. In general, MailChimp has a very user-friendly interface that makes the process of learning simple. It also has an opt-in form that is external that allows you to customize the permission forms. The form will be stored by MailChimp on its MailChimp website.

MailChimp offers three on-site opt-in forms, as well. For creating your own email messages, MailChimp offers a wide selection of templates for design as well as self-made styles in its Marketing Campaign Builder feature. The company also provides simple but effective autoresponder management tools as well as an excellent spam management tool called The Inbox Inspector. The features for tracking aren't as thorough as Aweber's however, they're still useful. Support from MailChimp's team is very helpful however, they are a bit restricted.

AWeber provides a one month trial for just $1, which is refundable in the event that you are not satisfied with the product. Their interface is highly effective and displays all of the data you require to be aware of about your marketing strategy directly in front of you through their website dashboard. There are a variety of form layouts and templates for letters to create your marketing messages. They are all very customizable.

AWeber also provides opt-in forms for customers to sign up to grant your business the right to send them email messages. The built-in opt-in feature makes it easy and quick for customers of yours to sign up to your emails. There are some users who have issues using the text editor of AWeber to make their e-mails, particularly when they copy and paste their e-mails written in other programs like Microsoft Word. The program does offer a wide variety of e-mail templates available that you can choose from however. The autoresponder management tools of AWeber give users the opportunity to get into more advanced methods of managing databases.

The spam management software from AWeber has a 99 percent success rateand comes with it with the Spam Score feature that allows users to determine the likelihood that your email will be categorized as spam. Their tracking tools are one of the best in the market and makes it easy to keep track of your plan. Their support staff is accommodating as well.

Constant Contact also has an excellent speed of delivery and is believed to be extremely user-friendly. It's blocked from military addresses, but this is something to think about in case you plan to sell to the military. They offer a 2-month trial at no cost and their pricing policy is similar to MailChimp as well as AWeber. It is also possible to design templates, monitor your marketing strategy and master the basics through webinars and instructional videos.

All of these automated email marketing tools can greatly increase the efficiency of your email marketing method. The three are relatively similar in price that means you'll be capable of determining which you should use based on the degree to which you like their user interfaces and also their design and design software. It is possible to trust each of them to send your emails in a timely manner and avoid being caught in the filtering of spam by your customers.

For the beginner in e-mail marketing with a small email list, MailChimp will be your best choice. Their free service for customers who have less than 12,000 email messages per month and less than 2000 addresses for e-mail will last forever and gives you 99percent of the features that paying customers enjoy.

MailChimp will also expand as you expand your e-mail marketing campaign is successful. Marketers looking to get into more advanced and intricate methods of e mail marketing may choose to use AWeber.

E-Mail Best Practices in Marketing

Here are some helpful tips to make sure that your email advertising campaign will be as effective as it can be.

Make sure you pay attention to the preview of your email

A majority of users will decide to open or block it according to the information in the subject line as well as your email address. Be sure to make your sender's name prominent and easily identifiable. Do not make your e-mail appear like it was sent by an automated giant.

The aim is to have your customers be able to recognize your brand to let them know who sent the email. The more trust the recipient has in your brand name, the more likely they'll read your email. Your subject line must be clear and concise in describing the contents of the email that makes the reader want to learn more about the information and thus decide to open the email.

Make sure your emails are easily accessible

Images with vibrant colors can be beneficial in enhancing the appearance and feeling of marketing emails however, make sure your emails are readable without images. Do not include images that have to be downloaded off the internet. This is because a huge portion of your users will be able to read and open your emails via mobile devices.

If the images downloaded do not show on mobile devices, your message might appear odd. If this happens, your client likely won't read your email. Make sure to use plain text in your email messages since it will look great across every platform.

* Make sure you have a high deliver rate by avoiding unwanted emails

You'll want to keep a the highest rate of delivery for your email messages to keep your clients interested. In order to do this, you need to make sure you don't get labeled spammer.

This is a good time to check with your e-mail provider to ensure you're not sending out many messages, and staying clear of the typical warnings about spam in your headings as well as subject line. (Such as"free" "free", "$$$$" and "You have won !!!! !") Don't get classified as spammers!

If possible you can personalize your email messages

Mail merging software which allows you to insert the name of the client into an e-mail generated by mass. Studies show that seeing their name on an email gives a sense of trust and confidence in the person receiving the message, which increases the likelihood that they read the email.

Make use of an automated email marketing tool

You can pick one of the top three AEMTs, or pick among the many other businesses that are on the market. The cost of these instruments is worth the value you receive in return.

It's nearly impossible to manage an extensive email marketing campaign using these methods. It's harder to monitor the results of your campaigns without these tools, too.

* Make your email content more personal

People want to be connected with the businesses they work with. If you are able to build an intimate relationship with your customers, chances are that you will earn the trust of their loyalty, respect, and repeat business. There is no one who would like to read a computer-generated email, so add some personality in it.

You can discuss your company's objectives and employees, charitable contributions and personal things. Include content about your hobbies, family and interests if you choose to. Create a relationship to your customers via your e-mail marketing campaigns.

A Sample list of Email Marketing Headlines:

* * "Announcing a new real estate listing" (Real Estate Company)

* "Bring an additional person to class during the week" (Dancing Studio Company)

* "Buy 1 and get 1 free Coffee Everyday!" (Coffee House)

* "See live owls in the wild during the weekend" (Wildlife Centre for Education and Shelter)

* "Check out our fitness club every week, risk-free" (Gym)

* "Get the second pair of glasses for free or glasses once you buy the latest pair" (Eyeglasses Corporation)

* * "New Model Showcase" (RV Dealership Company)
* "Dedicated Health Plans available to all Families" (Health Care Insurance Company)
* "Need an overhaul of the kitchen?" (Home Remodeling Company)
* "Earn energy Efficiency Tax Credits" (Window Company)
* "Four brand new wine releases this week" (Wine Shop)
* "We remove your old furniture free of charge" (Junk Removal company)
* "Brand Name Watches for Sale for Customers who are Valued" (Watch Corporation)
* "JJ's BBQ Unveils Its Hottest Sauce Ever!" (BBQ Restaurant)

Chapter 4: Making A Huge Email List

Making an email-list is the very first step to achieving successful marketing via email. The more extensive the list greater and more effective, it has chance of making money through the reach of individuals. It is true that many people get wrong when creating their email list by doing just one thing: picking random emails from any source. A few people have failed the marketing approach by picking the contacts on their lists and then asking their friends to send them more emails from their acquaintances. There are a variety of sites where you can receive emails, and some include social media accounts like Facebook or LinkedIn. Although you can attract a small number of people by using this method but the reality is that the majority of people will not even think about it, which makes your efforts pointless. The time needed to look through different profiles obtain emails, put them in databases, and duplicate them whenever you send emails is already exhausting and the fact that it won't yield the results you want is what makes this strategy useless.

What is the best option?

The only thing you have to do is make sure that the list that you build only contains addresses of those who are willing to sign up for the service you offer and to receive the marketing messages which are included. The advantages that come from having a list like this include that not only are those who subscribed willing to hear from you, it indicates that they are keen on what you're selling or nature of the service you offer. Geoff Roberts, an email marketing expert, claims that the best mailing lists have two key elements that are the offering of worth to website visitors and the development of a user-friendly experience that will benefit the people who use the service. 3. Once you have the complete list of potential users for your service, it's easy to interact with them, promote your service and even solicit their opinions on whatever it is that you're working on.

The following is a step by step instruction on how to make a professional email list.

Find Your Goal

Setting goals is among the most essential and crucial aspects of marketing via email. Before beginning any type of marketing there is a need to determine the direction your campaigns should follow so that you set clear goals and a measure of the success for your entire work. Additionally is having a plan ensures that you're working towards something you know about and that means you're not sending emails solely to make a point. Usually the objectives that have been clearly stated are not just a way for an organization to expand, but also act as a an incentive for all those who are involved.

Before you can write down any goals you have set you must be aware of areas of your business that might require improvement and help and also the key areas that you're than you are to invest in. There are currently four crucial tools that will aid you in assessing your company and assist you in making the best choice about the best strategy for your company. Email marketing is an important element of your business and the tools listed below can provide the required details that will allow you not only think on the best method of operation, but also assess the efficacy of your choices. When you've figured out the most relevant areas of your company, setting goals becomes a breeze.

1. SWOT Analysis of goals that are SMART

This SWOT analysis instrument is a crucial element in competitive market analysis and can also assist in narrowing the scope of your concepts until one can find a single goal they can concentrate on, which will allow their company to grow and expand in line with. When you employ this SWOT analysis tool it will not only be able identify one goal that you can achieve and achieve it, but you'll be able to make sure that you are able to compete with advantage that could increase the efficiency of your business.

Before you begin an SWOT analysis, it is important to be aware that different the businesses you work with are different.

This means you need to be able to narrow down the goals you wish to achieve to ensure that you obtain the best results. If you're just beginning and are not sure how to proceed, it might be beneficial to study other email marketers who have already proficient. In this way, you'll have a clear plan and you can make your way to ensure that you're doing things the right method. If you're not an expert and are not sure what to do, it is sensible to choose five companies in your industry which are thriving in the area of email marketing and to study their methods in order to tweak your own to make sure you are able to stand out. For instance, if are looking to drop ship choose a company that is skilled, like Shopify and try to examine their processes.

The third step is signing to receive newsletters. This will permit you to receive their emails, which will allow you to study the content and also show how these companies employ in their marketing through email. This analysis that you could be able to identify crucial elements that can assist you with your marketing plan. Once you have identified the strategies that you believe as the most effective and appealing, you'll be able narrow your objectives to the tactics you'd like to implement for yourself. There are generally six fundamental elements that make up your email marketing strategy:

* Mail frequency. How often do you want to send out emails to your customers? Daily? Weekly? Monthly? Annually?

"The subject line. What is the way in which the subject line written? Are the words catchy? Does it make you want to do something?

* What is the style for the magazine? Do you have a customized design employed? What factors influence your decision to sign up to the newsletter, or how you perceive the content? The design is analyzed on the basis of colors, the branded template as well as the typefaces.

* The images and their alignment with the text contained in the newsletter. How do they influence or aid in the growth of your interest?

* The degree at which the device is mobile-friendly. At present, more than 75% of smartphone users check their email on the phone, which requires the guarantee that their devices are compatible.

* Personalization levels. Examine the different levels and methods to ensure that senders send personalized emails to their recipients.

After you've analyzed each of these elements and analyzed them, you're in a better position to pinpoint the exact objectives you'll be working to, which will help you to execute your plan in the best way possible. To further refine your emailing goals the SWOT analysis is the next step. Before beginning the actual research make sure that the objectives are achievable.

Goals for email marketing that are SMART are essential as they guarantee that you are not at the chance of failing and not reaping the real and genuine advantages of the tool for marketing. It stands that stands for Specific, Measurable realistic, actionable, and Time-bound.

Concerning Specificity In terms of Specificity, the goal of email marketing must always be as fundamental the ability to deal with one specific issue. For example, you can focus on a higher number of subscribers, which results in higher sales, less bounce rates, and even lower complaints about spam. Whatever issue you're trying to solve make sure there is no confusion and that you're dealing with the problem that you are addressing. So, instead of stating that you are aiming for something abstract like "improvement of email performance" you could reduce it to something like "increase the number of subscribers by 10 percent."

In the case of measurability, this means that the goals that are specific must be able to be measured. In the case of the previous example that of increasing the subscriber count by 10 percent is already a measurability level which is the number value that is attached to the goal. When you assign the value a certain number, you are able to strive to ensure that you reach your objectives with a specific outcome with a clear goal in mind

Actionability in email marketing includes setting objectives to assist in improving their performance. Experts say that the best goals are those which continuously challenge you to be better with the capability to alter behavior and correct issues. If goals are fixed and unchangeable There is no reason to pursue them, and they'll ultimately cause your plans fall short. As an example, even if you're determined to expand your list of contacts, you need to be ready to go the extra mile to correct any issues that occur. Building your list is definitely important, but planning and not being tied to a single objective that is not measurable against the performance of your business is much more important.

Realism is among the most essential aspects of setting goals. It is never a good idea to pursue a goal that is not achievable since it only leads to disappointment and more misery. When making your goals for your email marketing it is important to ensure the goal you're trying to accomplish is actually something that is able to be accomplished, and stay away from being too exaggerated. For example, if you're just beginning your email marketing campaign with no followers and a subscriber percentage is feasible as a lot of people are making the switch to the campaign for the very first time. If a more established business has its goals for subscribers to 300%, it's unrealistic and a waste of time business plan, which isn't just difficult to accomplish, but could result in the use on a significant amount of money that could have been used elsewhere. When you decide on your goals consider realism as much as you can to ensure that you're not chasing the wind

Make sure that your plan is based according to a set timeline. A time-bound goal is a good thing and means you've identified the exact time frame within which you intend to meet your goals, and are confident that the deadline you set is enough and that you can actually achieve success in your business. For instance, the requirement of an increase of 100% of subscribers in just two hours is not feasible. But if your goal is to have this number of subscribers in two months, the timeframe is reasonable and you will be able to achieve your goal very quickly.

Marketing through email is not difficult and most marketers are looking to accomplish similar objectives. If you don't have a clear idea of what your goals ought to be, here are some examples could be useful or can help you to create your personal.

The increase is seen within

Reduced within

When you have made sure that each goal are SMART, you will ensure that you'll have a high probability of achieving the goals.

After you narrow it down and pinpoint the precise objectives you would like to attain, you're at last able to perform a SWOT assessment. It is an abbreviation used to describe the strengths and weaknesses, as well as opportunities and threats that affect your thoughts. Most of the time the weaknesses and strengths are internal, meaning that it's the leverage that a company is able to leverage that allows it to achieve success in its ventures. The threat and opportunities are thought to be external that means the business does not control them and they have to be prepared to deal with them in order to ensure that negative effects are not felt.

SWOT Analysis

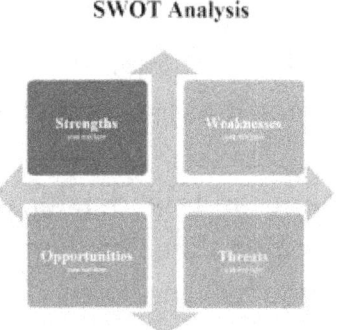

Figure 1. Diagram of the SWOT analysis.

The specific business each element in the SWOT framework can be different and distinct. But, there are many questions you could try to answer to help you to determine the different elements. In order to ensure that you receive all the relevant information and accurate, it is strongly recommended to include everyone who is employed within the company, as well as other stakeholders from outside like shareholders. When everyone brainstorms and participate in the identification of these elements, it is easy to determine all potential elements and discuss those that are most pertinent to your particular company.

Strengths

Examining the strengths of an organization is crucial since it assists in ensuring proper planning, taking decisions and management and leadership. Once you have identified the strengths of your business, you will be better equipped to design strategies that allow you to capitalize on these strengths, and to determine the measures that can help you increase the efficiency and effectiveness of these elements. Because you'll being discussing strengths and weaknesses of goals were identified as strengths in this instance there are greater chance of achieving and evaluation of the effectiveness and value of this objective. There are also many questions that will allow you to recognize these strengths. Some are:

* What are the areas we perform very well that can assist in the achievement of our goals?

In which aspects of our goal do we have a greater likelihood of beating current or potential rivals?

* What aspects will be crucial to the creation of revenue?

What advantages in the industry will assist in the accomplishment of your goal? For instance, if online rates are subsidised and you have the opportunity to earn quite well as an email marketing professional.

* What are the variables that are likely to aid the majority of tasks that generate revenue?

* How cooperative and committed is the team towards the achievement of the objective?

If you can answer the identified along with the relevant questions, you'll be able see the elements that will help you to make your goals stand out, allowing your company to be geared towards success.

The weaknesses

The opposite of weaknesses is strengths, and they assist in the identification of weaknesses and the challenges the business is confronting. In this scenario gaps are the identification of factors that could make your goal unattainable and, ultimately, could cause failure. When you recognize the weak spots then you'll be able to determine the possible mitigation strategies that will allow you to refine your goal and stop any possible impediment to achievement due to these weak points.

Some of the issues that will help you determine the weak points are:

• What could be some areas that could lead to a waste of resources to achieve the pursuit of

* What are the elements of the objective that can be made better?

* What elements and aspects that the company operates in could cause the failure of the objective? For example, if the goal is to send 1,000 emails in a single day, and you have only one technician that is not enough, then it could be too much and the target won't be achieved.

Once you have identified all the weak points, you can identify mitigation strategies. In the event that there aren't any fallback strategies then you can modify or try to find an alternative goal

Opportunities

As stated earlier, opportunities depend on external elements, and comprise of factors outside your control and will affect your business. When setting goals it is important to consider the opportunities that will help the achievement of your goals. Most of the time, opportunities exist only in the context of their surroundings and depend on factors like the sector one is in as well as your competitors' actions as well as other elements.

A few of the questions that will help you determine these opportunities include:

• What is one gaps or gaps within our industry that to fill?

* Which audience does this goal target as well as who are other audiences that the goal does not target but should be targeted?

How can we alter the purpose to make it more perfect and more precise to demands of the industry?

After you have answered such questions, you could discover the areas and other elements you might not have considered The end outcome is an increased chance to make improvements.

Threats

They are also external, meaning that the business doesn't have control over the way they occur. Threats are an undesirable event and recognizing these can help in the formulation of strategies to mitigate them and counteract them whenever they arise. If you don't take action to counter the threat, it could lead to the loss of your company or the overall goal.

A few of the questions you could ask yourself are:

* What elements of this plan are most risky? For example, sending email to thousands of people without having a clearly defined strategy is likely to have your email go to the spam folder.

* What will our prospective market think of our product and the objective we're trying to accomplish?

Since the threat is external, you might not be able to get all the answers you need from brainstorming. Therefore, it is essential to hold regular sessions following the accomplishment of the plan in order to understand the responses you're getting.

After you've confirmed that your goals are SMART , and improved them by using the SWOT assessment, you'll be able to ensure that you are on the right path and you can proceed to carry out the process.

Profile Your Audience

The audience is similar to the market that is targeted to email marketers. As per Rikke Thomsen, it is essential to always ask yourself these four questions to make sure you have a proper identification of the target demographics of the individuals who might benefit from the service or purchase the products. [4]

1. The Action: What is the Goal of the Campaign?

The purpose for the marketing campaign will be the initial and most important question you have to answer prior to any other considerations when selecting your target potential audience. In general, the goal of the campaign is to lead to the specific actions you want your subscribers to perform. Like any other form of marketing can be used in the following ways:

• increasing awareness of the availability and presence of the product

* increasing sales in areas where numbers aren't high.

* registering more participants when needed

* the preparation stage where a brand new product will be manufactured

Once you have identified the motive and purpose for which you'd like to start the campaign, you will be clear regarding the corresponding procedure. Most of the time, there will be different strategies taken to address the various calls to actions and the more clear the purpose is, the simpler you will determine the best way to accomplish it in the situation. Think about the scenarios below and the various actions they intend to make.

If the objective is to create awareness of the availability and presence of an item, the ultimate goal of the strategy could be to increase sales, so an appealing advertisement is needed. Therefore, the purpose of the advertisement is to grab the attention of potential customers which will allow your product to become a household brand and to become well-known. Service providers are those that are seeking recognition in order that users can search for the services they need when they require them. For instance, dropshipping businesses strive at reaching as wide a range of potential customers as they can, demonstrating to prospective customers how easy the service will be. In this scenario when a customer wants to buy or import something online, they will know that they can choose to work with the company and avoid the hassle of having to organize the shipping of the items themselves. The demand is for potential buyers to make use of the service or promote it to friends.

If the aim is to attract the maximum number of registrations then the business can employ techniques like grabbing the attention of prospective users by providing a small amount of information, and then requiring the users to sign up for a particular service in order that they will be able to access all the information. It is not uncommon to find a website that grabs your attention by asking you to answer several questions before they can inform you of the outcome, for instance, by answering five questions regarding your eating habits in order to provide you with the best ways to shed weight. If you're trying to shed weight, this process will immediately draw your attention. You'll have to answer five questions, and when receiving the answer, you'll have to sign-up and include an email address so that results are sent to it. In this instance the "call to action" is to encourage interested users to register and you'll be able to achieve your goal.

If the goal is to get ready in advance for the unveiling of a brand new item, launchers could be trying to create the maximum amount of interest they can in order that people will be intrigued and look for the announcement. When there is a buzz towards the unveiling and launch of a product there is a likely chance of generating more sales, which implies that businesses will ultimately invest significantly less on marketing. The demand for action is to get people who are interested in using the product to anticipate the announcement of the product and, if they are successful, increase sales.

With these three scenarios in mind it's evident that clarity of the ultimate purpose is essential. Call to Action to those who may be interested in becoming participants and users of whatever you're selling should be simple and straightforward since that's the only method by which the majority of them will be involved.

2. The Targeted Audience: Who Is the Campaign aimed at?

After you've identified the specific actions you would like the various users to perform It is important to identify the individuals that you can involve. This is the intended people, who could have different requirements for involvement. That's where discernment comes into play when the list is long You can use electronic tools to aid you. In particular, it would not seem sensible to send everyone who is on the list an invitation email, since some people have already registered. Additionally, certain services offer free trials to users who are new. This is why it doesn't be beneficial to distribute to everybody coupons for trial, since some people have tried it out and are currently using the paid service. When you exercise discernment and make the right choices, you not only demonstrate professionalism, but you also try to provide the value they deserve, thus increasing your chance of having a good interactions.

For a good example of audience targeting you can think of an online service like Netflix. The streaming platform is considered to be one of the top companies that are winning in the field of email marketing due to its high degree of personalization meaning that the advertisements are sent out to various people aren't random to say the most cases, but are designed for each person and their uniqueness. When you sign for an account, the messages that you receive pertain to a free trial of 30 days that allows you to stream unlimited amount of content for no cost. Additionally, the company asks that you select a handful of films and shows you enjoyed when signing in, which allows them to determine the genre of films you are drawn to. When you sign up, the majority of the emails you get correspond to possible movies you might like, using the movies you have selected from your selection as a predicative element. This means that the service does not deliver the same predictions to all users, but tailors the content of the emails according to the distinct preferences of various people. If this is the case it becomes easy for someone to find an interest in the service and log on to go to the films. In the end, the benefits will last beyond the trial time, and those who are targeted are more likely to becoming a subscriber to the paid subscription.

Also, in keeping with the audience you are targeting it is important to understand that more and more people are accessing their emails via their phone, as opposed to computer or desktop. Therefore, you must ensure that whatever format you decide to use to distribute your ads is compatible with computers and phones.

3. The Benefit: What's the value to Subscribers?

Value for the subscribers is achieved when the targeted market is able to take the action you asked them to. As the initiator or sender you are aware of the impact that the success in executing the request to act has on you. In the event that more people sign up it is likely that you'll see an increase in sales, which means an increase in revenue for you. This being said however, there is another important requirement you need to meet: the benefits to your subscribers. A good relationship must have mutual interest, and this isn't any more than that. Consider the other subscribers in the process, and try to give them something of benefit.

Service providers will surely have a much easier time demonstrating the benefits their services provide to their clients. In the case of an app like Netflix the benefit that consumers is access to unlimited movie streaming for the same cost. Furthermore, the fact users have the option to pick their preferred package will mean that they only pay for what they require. If you're typically busy and your spare time is perhaps on weekends, you could opt for the basic plan that is less expensive. If you're a person with lots of time, and want to be able to spend hours watching films, the more advanced packages will be sufficient.

Additional examples of the value or value you can offer your customers are:

* Direct access to service providers after registration. Customers can contact the service providers with any questions and seek assistance anytime of the day. support staff will be available to assist.

• One-month of unlimited access to our services without cost

* 20% off on the first two purchases you make

Delivery is free of items when purchased within a period of two days

It is clear that people prefer to feel that they're the ones in charge, and that they are the ones that have benefited from an interaction far more than other people. When you include keywords like FREE or DISCOUNT, it gives the impression that the customers benefit, and they could be more likely to sign up for the service in comparison to other times. As an email marketing specialist make use of this opportunity to earn the trust of subscribers, which will help keep them loyal and ensure that they will actually utilize the paid services in the future. Similar to Netflix the moment a user has seen a lot of movies without buffering issues from the website they're likely to to buy the service after the trial period has ended. If this occurs it's evident that email marketers are successful in their endeavor.

4. These Results: What is the measure of success in the campaign?

Now you've determined the best option as well as the advantages you can expect to get once your customers take the actions you would like to see them take. It is now time to establish the indicators that will help towards achieving those goals.

For certain companies those who believe that the best results are fairly straightforward as it is determined by rate of subscribers as well as those who click. In other cases, the number of sales coming from those who received the emails is an excellent indicator of the results, but these people only examine the sales figures.

Your measurement of the results you get must be simple and this is the only method by which you'll be able to profit from the marketing strategy and determine which strategies are effective and which isn't. Also that businesses have different goals and different results means that the measurement of your success is likely to be different. Therefore, don't use the standard used by other companies, instead create your own.

If you can answer those four concerns, you'll be able to see a better picture of your audience potential, allowing you to take appropriate action and strive to satisfy their desires.

Create a Website

I'm not able to stress enough on the necessity for email marketers to have an online presence. If you're conducting email marketing for someone else ensure that the person has their own site that you can operate from. Nowadays, making websites is easy and inexpensive, and every excellent email marketer owns one.

Some people might believe that only those who are subscriptions to paid services should have websites. But this could be more wrong. It doesn't matter what it is you're working with. Making sure you have a site that visitors are able to look over the issues you face will not only give your business an upscale appearance, and enables visitors to be more discerning about your company. Assuming you're an author with a team you manage and writing to potential prospects and telling them how great of your writer you are might not be enough. But, if you are on the web, customers will be able to look around, view examples, and then make their own minds as to whether you are a good fit for their professional criteria.

In some cases, there's a reason that you'll want to start sending emails without having an online presence. For certain people, they may not have enough funds to invest in a customized website while for others it might be due to a inexperience of managing an online presence. Whatever reason you have consider that it's still feasible to become an effective email marketing professional without websites. If you're such someone, I recommend that you get an online presence as soon as you are able to. For now, you can use the following strategies for your marketing efforts.

1. Direct visitors to your business social media sites

The web is now full of activity and is continuing to open the doors of many individuals who want to be successful in various areas in their life. Popular websites like Facebook or Instagram have provided opportunities for entrepreneurs, as well as for everyone who would like to put their work out there and should make sure there is at minimum a professional account. For instance, if work as a graphic designer, make sure you have social media accounts that showcase your work and you should work to gain an audience on these sites prior to attempting marketing via email. Instagram is the ideal platform for those who promote digital products or would like to market their business to different marketing agencies. After you've polished your Instagram websites to the best possible quality add URLs to the pages in your email marketing campaigns. The most important thing is to ensure that you've got a solid call to action that keeps people interested and connected to your business.

2. Make sure that potential visitors are kept informed by providing new information

The best benefits of having your own website is that you don't need to keep your users informed of new content. All you need to do is post updates on your site and they can view it whenever they visit the websites. Without having a website, it is ever more complicated and you need to make sure that prospective customers and followers are kept informed regarding any new product or service you create. Typically, service providers and those who are involved in events like public speaking could benefit from this option since they need to keep their audience updated with the latest discussions, topics, venues and payment options as well as dates. Don't just provide information, but rather to get an immediate response from people who read your blog. If you are a public speaking community and those who love public speaking, the best method of doing so is to convince a lot of people to join.

3. Offer special deals and incentives like coupons and discounts

We all enjoy free stuff and getting things that are valuable for less than market value. So, try to grab potential customers' and readers at their attention by offering exclusive discounts and increase the likelihood of receiving an immediate response. For example giving 20% off your first purchase will not just make the recipient happy with the email, but also encourage them to take a look at the social media sites to which you have redirected them to in order to determine if they have something you'd like to see. This is the reason that worldwide black Fridays on online stores are time of year that retail sales hit their peak numbers.

Absolutely, marketing via email is much easier if you have an online presence. If you don't already have one, try getting one in the shortest time possible.

Email Marketing Services

There's no doubt that you are aware of the fundamentals of email marketing and how it could assist your business in growing. But there are occasions that you aren't sure the best way to approach it, or perhaps you're so involved in various other things that you do not have the time or energy to perform these services. In such a case the best option is to seek the services of email marketers from reputable companies with a reasonable cost. There are currently numerous online marketing firms offering email marketing services for a minimal cost and you are able to select the one that interests you.

There are numerous benefits to using email marketing among them:

The firm will inform you on the best way to go about your business that will help you expand your list significantly and will provide you with insight into the things you may not have considered.

* The fact that the majority of the businesses are in operation for quite a while means they've identified important points that can aid you in getting the best from your products and services.

The marketing services perform all the work. The tiny amount you pay can't be compared to the enormous benefits you can reap.

* Lastly, you will have an opportunity to learn by studying the way service providers work so that in the future, you'll be able conduct your marketing with professionalism.

Call to Action (CTA)

Call to action is regarded as the ultimate piece of art that makes the ideal email marketing strategy stand out from the rest. It is important to note that so far as buttons for call-to-action have to be distinctive which means that they must be prominent and feature appealing texts, the reality is that they're more than they are. Effective email marketers don't abandon the task to operate on their own and in isolation, but instead think of it as an ending which makes the entire marketing idea and output engaging and captivating. Similar to a narrative the CTA must be based on the same structure of drawing people into the story by building it up and ending by telling it the most engaging way possible. The way people react will be according to how you end up selling the story, so it is essential to ensure that it is as flawless and flawless as is possible. The more reactionsyou get, the more extensive your final checklist will become.

One of the most important things you need to put some consideration into is the layout and the precise location where you should place your calls to action. If your newsletter has many themes that have numerous calls to action, be sure that the areas are aligned to one to each other. This is a call-to-action which has been strategically located in a suitable location which increases the likelihood of gaining customers and increasing sign-ups

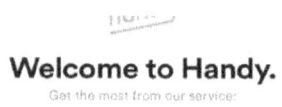

Figure 2. Illustration of a well-designed call to take action.

It is clear that the button was carefully placed underneath the welcome sign. This allows prospective customers with an the desire to sign up without the hassle of needing to search for the login symbol again. Psychologically speaking, people are able to read in a linear fashion from the left, and from top to bottom, placing the sign-up link at the bottom of the sign-up page extremely effective.

Remember that your customers may not be focusing at the CTA link if you've added additional links to the same spot. In reality, they could be enticed by additional buttons, which could derail your goal to have them sign up just. This is why you should ensure that you only have one button on your landing page. As can be seen from the the image above there is only one button. This means that users will only have one decision to make. If you've got additional links you believe could be useful to viewers, you can place them elsewhere away in the distance from your CTA button. You can also offer readers a hint of other links and then redirect your visitors towards the CTA button and require them to sign up first before accessing the content. Redirecting is a common practice on a lot of sites and asking users to sign-up first will see your subscriber list expanding dramatically in the shortest amount of time.

Make an Offer

Making an offer was covered in detail in earlier sections. This aspect involves offering something to people for free and thereby gaining their attention and influencing them towards achieving what you want to accomplish. Offer discounts, coupons and deals to be able to attract the attention of many individuals, without doubt.

Make sure that you enable Content Sharing

Many times, you've been told about materials and content becoming viral. The reason this happens is because of the sharing power, which means that people come across something they like and then share it with their circle of friends, a few of whom then share the content. In the end, more people are exposed to the content than originally expected, which results in an increase in awareness of the issue. For instance, if you're selling your items at a discounted price of 50 certain people will be happy to the point where they would like all their friends to be aware so that they can all shop together. In the end, other friends will pass the link on to their friends and, in the end you'll have more sales, and more visitors to your site. The more people sign up and sign up, the bigger your list grows. So, no matter what you're dealing with, ensure that your content can be shared.

Additionally, encourage people to follow and share your content prior to your CTA because they might not be aware there is a way to share your content. The more people who share, the better.

Common Email Marketing Errors to avoid

It is clear that marketing via email remains among the most effective options especially for the small-scale business owner. The advantages of email marketing are not in doubt, and range from engaging with the target audience to increasing readership among potential clients as well as significantly increasing revenue for an extremely low cost. It is also believed to be extremely simple for the majority of people, that makes it a great choice for virtually every business. However, there are several common errors that hinder the full possibilities of email marketing that are committed by a wide range of marketers who use email. A few of these errors include:

1. Infractions to Email Marketing Regulations and Stipulations

As with any other enterprise or company there are a variety of terms and conditions that govern any platform. The sending of emails to a particular list is not restricted, but you should be aware the conditions of use for several of the most popular email platforms require these large-scale messages to be sent direct to the mailers folder. For these companies it is essential to make sure that the individuals whom you send the emails to have signed up to whatever you're selling, which is similar to giving permission to receive these documents. Additionally, all emails should contain a prominent and clearly visible opt-out button. You must comply with this rule to prevent being bombarded with emails. In addition, the more you are contacted by spammers and the less you can decrease your credibility to prospective clients which can result in a near failure of your campaign. Personally, there's an organization whose email address I receive every day in my junk mail folder. So far, I think of the company as negative and never accept anything from them as seriously. Don't make this error again.

2. Not Being Friendlier to Subscribers

Marketing via email, like other methods of marketing, is mostly about sweet talk and persuading potential clients that they'll take the desired move. In addition, adding more subscribers on your list of email recipients is a great thing. However, you should not stop there. In the same way you tried to gain new subscribers, make sure that you put in as much effort to keep your existing subscribers.

So, what's the best option?

Personalization is among the methods you can use to not only get to know the new members, but also let them feel valued by them. If and whenever one feels appreciated, they are more likely to remain. It is an established fact that a space in which you don't feel valued is not appealing to you in the least. Your customers are exactly the same. If they feel appreciated They will definitely remain with you. This is equally true. These are the ways you can make your subscribers feel appreciated and welcomed:

* Addressing them with their first name. I've signed up to several newsletters and publications. When these newsletters contact me by name, it gives me an overwhelming feeling connectedness and acceptance. The newsletters I receive make me want to go through the content of the message, and I'm more likely to act whenever it is required. This is in contrast to emails that are targeted at me in general and do not give me a feeling of being part of the group. In such instances I'm less likely to take an interest which means that I have a low chance of actions. I'm certain that a lot of customers are just like me so I would strongly suggest to utilize functions that automatically enter name of subscribers.

* You must engage with your customers frequently, not only when you have coupons or newsletters that you want to distribute. Certain email marketers require

their subscribers to enter specific information like dates of birth, making it possible to track the birthdays of these subscribers. Additionally, these marketers need to input the nationality of their subscribers that allow them to keep track of important occasions like holidays in these countries. With this information, websites send birthday wishes and emails with happy holidays to those who are relevant and make them feel comfortable and at the home of their customers. If you're in the process of doing so, you're very much lagging behind in the loyalty of your customers.

3. Not Taking the Time to include the Call-to-Action

As we have already discussed, the significance of the call-to action button cannot be overemphasized. Be sure to follow the principles discussed in the past including securing it on your own landing page, without any other websites.

4. Not Enough Emails to Send

The fact that people sign up to your blog doesn't give you the authority to bombard users with emails or send them numerous emails every day. For instance, a typical user receives an average of one hundred and 121 emails per day and that's more than 44,000 emails over the course of a year. If you're among those who are bombarding other people with numerous emails, you can are an annoying nuisance, eventually leading those who receive these emails to unsubscribe from your email newsletter. In a study that took place by Quicksprout more than 46.4 percent of subscribers who unsubscribed were due to receiving excessive emails from the various sites they had signed up to. Five other factors that led to people not subscribing to emails are illustrated in the image below.

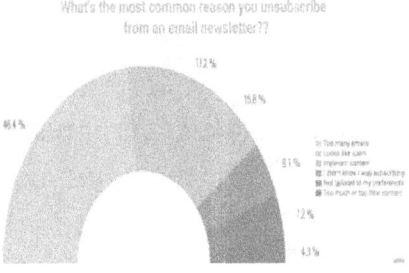

Figure 3. Illustration of the reason why that the majority of subscribers do not opt-out of content. [6]

This chart does a great job of summarizing the other mistakes you should avoid. As you can see, the other reason why the vast majority of subscribers did not sign up was that the message appeared to be spam. In chapter 3, you'll discover how the majority of messages are discarded being thrown into the junk mail folder as well as some of the steps you can take to ensure your messages don't end up in the spam folder.

In the diagram, marketers who require you to sign up to specific information and then frequently sending you irrelevant content is a different problem. For example, you could join the weight loss newsletter, which you expect to send you information on healthy living and eating. If when you start receiving newsletters from the website about plastic surgery. However but the information becomes boring and readers eventually cease to be interested. In addition, there are numerous opportunities for earning money online in the space, some of which include advertising and marketing. If you lure customers into downloading certain types of information and then begin to provide them with content that is that is related to different forms of marketing, you're making a mistake and sooner or sooner you'll lose your subscribers.

Find an equilibrium and make sure that you're not giving out too much or too little content. A large amount of output has been discussed, leaving us with a lack of information. If you've signed up to a newsletter, for whatever reason, it's obvious that you'd want to receive updates periodically. Imagine subscribing to a wellness publication, and then receiving updates every month. This is not enough and doesn't benefit anyone over the long term. Find an equilibrium.

Chapter 5: How To Optimize Your Marketing Via Email

Marketing via email is among the tools that are used by the majority of general marketers. It is clear that email marketing isn't just utilized for engaging with your audience, as well as to generate leads, as well as increasing sales and interaction with prospective clients. The way to achieve the success of email marketing is not only achieved when you have a huge list of customers you are able to send out emails to, but instead by making them take note of the various calls to actions. Obviously, email marketers only focus on open rates as well as click-through rate since these are their only numbers that are important. What can you do to improve your email so that they're both excellent and also get the reader to read and open the emails, while ignoring other emails? This chapter will guide you through the process of optimizing email marketing, regardless of whether you're just starting out or an expert to help you achieve the best results from the same.

Define the Objective of Your Campaign

In case you're not aware the point that having a clear objective is among the most important elements of marketing via email. The subject has been covered extensively in the chapter 1 and I would suggest that you revisit or read through the most important aspects to review what you've learned. Without having a concise and precise objective, it is difficult to move forward effectively.

Find a fascinating subject

The next most important aspect after having a clear purpose is to have a compelling subject line. Usually, the headline is often the very first element people who receive the email will see. The extent to which it is interesting to them determines if they decide to decide to open it or ignore. Don't be obvious and do not make it boring. Today, users are able to access a variety of publications online as well as on their various social media accounts and the only thing that can determine which publications they'll access is the degree that the caption entices them.

Be aware that providing a compelling topic isn't clickbait. Don't lie about the subject line in order to get people to click your links as it could lead to a the loss of trust, and when it happens, you'll lose your subscribers.

Some of the ways that have been proved to add some excitement to subjects are:

* Incorporate your subscriber's name in order to ensure that they feel as if you're speaking to them directly. For instance, "Michael, would you want to know how to make websites?" One of the advantages of asking a direct inquiry is the fact that it prompts an answer, thereby inducing those who receive the messages to take a conscious choice to either decide whether or not they want to take the call to actions. Also, asking questions generates interest and boosts the probability of them heeding the appeal to action.

Make sure that the front load contains only crucial words. When people are reading the highlights or subjects of magazines or newsletters in the process, they instantly make their minds as to whether or not the information is relevant in their lives or not. Thus, make sure the most important words are obvious on first glance. For example, if you're specialization is diet and food include terms like healthy, long-lived weight loss, long life and other such. It's also important to consider that people usually love deals, which is why you should include terms like low-cost, cost-free, or discounts. A good instance of the subject line containing crucial words would be: .

In the above example above, the email marketer has distributed an exact amount of recipes, which makes the reader feel like they are going to benefit of the information. Additionally, words like as "guarantee" convey the impression that you have faith that you are adamant about what you wrote. So, the readers stand a more confidence in that you are a trustworthy source. Furthermore, telling them that you'll see them losing weight in just two weeks can be a more compelling incentive and can motivate them to check out your newsletter.

Importantly, it is important to provide personalization, and reminding the readers that they're the intended audience. To ensure personalization, make sure you include a subject line that is comprised of personal pronouns like "your," "you," or the individual's name. For example: .

• Finally, make sure you are sure to be clear. Clarity is among the most crucial elements of marketing via email, and shouldn't be compromised even the slightest. Be aware that most people have a small attention span, which means the necessity of being concise in your message and to concentrate on bringing the message home. Always make sure to stay clear of lengthy content which can confuse readers and cause their depletion of interest.

Determine the sender of your Email

A major and crucial and crucial aspects of marketing via email is to build trust with readers. That's why the name of the sender is one of the most crucial elements that allow readers to know quickly who they are receiving emails from. The sender of the email plays significant influence in determining who the recipients would like and do not want to receive email from. It has been said in the past, people get thousands of messages from various individuals on a daily basis and it's an ongoing process of separating those emails you'd prefer to read from the ones you would not like to. Be sure your name is one that people would like to hear from by optimizing your name to create a level of trust and a relationship with the people who read it. A few ways in which you can efficiently enhance your name include:

Send emails from an actual person rather than to a business name. For example, one of the emails that I receive that I usually am looking forward to comes from a company that writes, which I will identify as X. The company doesn't send out emails under the name of the business, but rather from different individuals who have access to the information. For example, if the message concerns policies or payments The emails come from Cullen, X company. If it's a marketing message and the email addresses show the sender's name with the name Paul, X company. This level of personalization not only do I feel grateful for the effort that all employees of the company spend to share a range of information however, I am capable of identifying the specific kind of message that is sent simply from the title. Typically, identifying who sent the email creates a warm and personal style, ultimately confirming the idea that the message originates from a real person and not a machine.

Note that getting your right senders is not an easy task, and you'll need to run several tests to determine which best draw the attention of the readers. Take for instance the rate of clicks in the case of the CEO , as contrast to when the sender is a marketing manager. What are the most popular emails that people are reading? If you have the right data, you'll be able to utilize this information to the best advantage.

* Lastly, you must make sure that you have a reply-to email address that is managed by a real person. We've all encountered websites run by bots, but the experience isn't as great as the experience of websites operated by real individuals. If you provide a reply-to email address gives your customers the impression that real people will be contacting the site, which can be crucial to increase trust and make your marketing more efficient.

Personalize Your message

As mentioned, personalization is crucial as it enhances the importance to the message. According to a study from 2018 which took place by MarketingSherpa approximately four out of 10 email messages considered spam were because people who received them believed that they were be insignificant. 7] To make sure that your emails have the impression of being more personal it is important to personalize your message. Make it clear to your subscribers that you truly care about them and, to a certain extent, have a sense of their personalities. Be extremely cautious with the kind of information you decide to influence subscribers by using. This is an example of personalization and usage of customer data done correctly, and the website will definitely catch the attention of these people immediately.

Figure 4. Illustration of a personal message. [8]

As you can tell from this instance, the business did not just send an unintentional message to the subscriber. It is rather, it is filled with relevant information that can make the reader think and more likely to engage in the services being provided. Fortunately, accessing some of this data, such as your number of fans your account has on Facebook is a breeze. All you have to do is to have your followers sign in to their social media accounts and then you can view the information accessible to everyone for free.

Be aware that there are certain information that may make subscribers scream and it wouldn't be wise to make use of the information even if it is available in the public domain. Some examples include:

* Number of children of the subscribers
* Names of children and immediate family members of subscribers.
* pointing to that the subscription address

It is important to note that personalization doesn't simply mean calling people by their name. Try to think outside the box and utilize filters to collect as much information about individuals as you can. In the present, you can engage third-party companies that offer surveillance capitalism services. they can assist you in narrowing down the needs of various people based on what they do on the internet. Based on this data you can personalize your emails to inform recipients that the email was made specifically for the audience.

Compelling Body Copy

The body text is the primary element of the email, and includes the components that compose the message. Be aware that this portion should be as short and as compelling as you can and is an element of an email that a lot of marketers focus on. When writing the body of your email, the most important factor to think about is to make it as engaging as you can. Simply, answer the following questions:

* What are ways to ensure that the copy sounds good?

* How can I make my appeal more compelling?

* Which tone of language or layout do I select?

After you've come up with some ideas about the best you can compose the text, be sure that every word that you wrote explains the value of the information and the reason the value of this information. Be sure to entice readers to the point that they are eager to continue reading the next paragraph. The first sentence is the most crucial aspect and will determine if readers will continue reading the content. Take a look at the next two sentences that discuss the same topic.

The two sentences discuss Prado's, the first one doesn't stir much interest when as compared to the other. After reading the first sentence there are a myriad of questions that immediately pop up in your head.

How do I learn more about the Prado's?
* What is wrong with it?
* What I know is one of the things that are incorrect?
• What should I know to fix this?

The fact that your interest is generated means that you'll be more inclined to read on, eventually achieving the purpose of an email marketing professional. Keep your messages short engaging and captivating Don't hesitate to employ vibrant words to get your message across. As much as you can to make your stories as short as possible with a focus on your use of bullet points.

Segmenting Your Subscribers

Segmenting subscribers is another essential aspect of marketing via email that can't be ignored. Particularly, targeted and segmented emails are not just the most effective ways to ensure that relevant content is delivered to those who require it most, but also increases the return on investment for the general email by more than 77%..

There are several known methods by which you can efficiently segment your customers. According to AWeber one methods for segmenting your subscribers include: [99

1. Inviting your customers to create profiles to allow you to discern certain information about their personal lives by analyzing their profiles. Profiles should include the most important information like contact numbers, birth date as well as nationality and any other information you believe is crucial to segmentation. After the segmentation data is finally

determined, you are free to utilize it however you like. In particular, ways you could make use of the information included in profiles of the users are:

* Sending out emails based on the various nations of your subscribers. Assuming you own an actual store located in the United States that you are selling, you should not expect anyone who lives in Africa to make the trek all the way to the United States to buy an product. Therefore, your filters must be limited to those who are actually residents of the United States and remove any other people off the list. For residents of other nations The best option is to promote online shops and perhaps identify their countries along with details about how you can ship items to them.

* Deliver the email according to the skills of the various users. For instance the abilities of users can range between intermediate, beginner and advanced levels. These kinds of skill sets typically are required in situations when you are offering an educational online courses, hence it is important to differentiate

between people who require assistance right from the start and those who need advanced instruction. This is crucial since it guarantees that every category of people is attended to, which makes people more interested in the topic.

2. Email campaigns and incentive campaigns that are based on significant dates for subscribers like their birthdays. There are certain periods of the year when people are happy to be appreciated and valued and valued, among them is birthdays. At this time it is possible to entice customers by not just wishing their birthdays a Happy Birthday, but also providing them with a quality service or product for free or at a reduced cost. If a person awakes to a message of happy birthday from a retailer and a 20 percent discount on purchases for the day, it's enough to motivate them and will lead them to purchase such products within a matter of minutes.

3. Emails containing more professional and business issues like webinars, for instance, to those who seem to likely be most

intrigued. Certain events are only considered important by a small number of people as not all people are involved in corporate activities, like participation in webinars. A few of those who are likely to be interested are the corporate managers in companies leader, as well as other individuals with control. If you have information like this in the profiles made by the participants, make use of it, and make sure you only send emails to these individuals. You can also send an email before inviting people to sign-up to determine if they are interested in the webinars coming up and then only send subsequent emails only to those who have expressed an interest.

4. The position of your sales funnel. Whatever you're working on You must remember that every one of the customers is searching for different things in your company, and the primary element that will determine their next steps is where they are within the funnel. There are different levels of the funnel and you should always try to determine the

subscriber's identity according to the location they are in. There are four phases: "The awareness" stage. In this stage the subscriber only recently discovered the company and its distinct functions, meaning that the brand is still relatively new to them. Since you're working with all subscribers and prospective subscribers online, it's vital to make sure that each of them has their requirements addressed. Additionally, the absence of interaction with a person means that you don't know what stage the person is in. So, you should treat all new customers as if they're in the awareness stage and try to resolve the issues that led them to your website as quickly as you could.

* The interest stage is followed the interest stage, and it is here that the potential customer base decreases. Because all the new customers were provided with information regarding the capabilities of the business at the earlier stage, this will determine whether or not they maintain the interest they have, based on the capability of the company to

address many of their issues. While the total number of potential customers is decreasing, the likelihood of conversion is significantly increased, and you have to find answers to questions from the customers whose interest remains high.

* The decision phase is the next step, and it is the point at which the customers have been informed of every function of the business. They can therefore make decisions about how they can participate in various aspects in the firm. In the case of sales, for instance are involved, customers will be able to choose when it comes to purchasing a specific product. You may be in a position to influence the choice of your subscribers by sending out emails consistently which attempt to provide the reasons for making a purchase decision best best and what benefits can be reaped by subscribers in the event of making the purchase.

The last stage is often referred to as the action stage and is thought to be a moment in which you will know the results of your efforts or not. If the person who subscribes is sufficiently convinced, they'll decide to purchase the item or subscribe to an item or service. Be aware that keeping customer loyalty and the possibility of future sales are crucial in this regard as well as one of the best methods to achieve both is to keep a constant track of the customer and encouraging customers who purchased the product to give them a rating and to tell them how the product or service could be improved.

Make the most of mobile Technology

Today mobile technology is considered to be one of the primary aspects of marketing via email. It is important to note that in the past, emails were mostly seen from personal computers. Since emailing was believed as professional, most people would check their emails working at home or for work-related projects. But things have changed and email is now being utilized just like other method of communication. The professional appeal is disappearing increasing numbers of people are browsing their emails at throughout the day via their mobile phones, since they aren't solely focused on work anymore. According to research, people will typically glance at their mobile phone and sign in to various social media websites just 30 mins after getting up. Email is one of those websites, which is why it is the importance of optimizing mobile devices for email marketers.

There are numerous ways to enhance mobile technology to ensure that your emails appear professional for phones with mobiles. The methods are:

1. Utilizing the Simple Design

One of the most effective strategies to optimize mobiles to email-based marketing involves to keep it simple, and employing simple designs that are simple to read. Everyone doesn't want a complicated layout which they don't understand how to go about reading and must deal with lots of confusion. Utilize the following design guidelines to make sure you're at the top of your game in the design process:

Clean up any obstructions that can lead to blurry hyperlinks. The basic principle of this advice is that less is better. It is better for the person who receives the email to be able to access smaller amounts of information than offering multiple links which will create confusion and eventually cause the recipient to give up on reading the content in the email altogether.

Make sure you set the font's size to adhere to the general rule of thumb with a minimum of 14 pixels in text, and 22 pixels on headlines. A font that is either too big or too small can make the text appear unprofessional and a large number of people might not even notice the information in it. In this case you'll miss the goal you set that is to get your message out to the maximum number of people possible.

* It is essential to know that the rules and features of operating systems like Android differ greatly from the rules of operating systems like Apple. Certain OSs will resize text automatically to ensure they appear appealing and easy to read on screens. In other OSs, you have to keep an eye on the text's dimensions. Because you don't know

the kind of OS that your users use It's best to adhere to the rules of the thumb.

2. Testing, Retesting, then then Test again

I cannot stress enough that you should test each of the functions in isolation to make sure they're precisely what you're looking for. Before you send emails to your subscribers, conduct an initial test by sending the message on several different devices. Examine the reader's ease of reading and the way that texts appear on your screen as that's the only way you will be able to determine what the readers will think of the message. If they don't interest you, the chances are that they won't be appealing to your readers either. Make sure to test and tweak until you're happy with the final product.

3. Your landing page is imperative

After you've completed the process of optimizing your marketing plan be aware that the most crucial thing you can do in this moment is to improve your landing page. Be aware that your website is the sole location that can give you the result you desire as it serves as a need to take the action. Be aware that improving efficiency is the aim for this particular situation and you need to be sure that any aspect like that the page takes a long time to load isn't ideal. Replace any data codes that are heavy you have more efficient code, and you'll have improved your landing page.

4. Utilizing the Responsive Template

If you're using a template that is predetermined by the provider of your email it is crucial to make sure that all of the information in it is responsive, meaning that it's not a fixed structure and can alter in accordance with the needs of the user, ensuring that texts appear the same no matter if you're using a smartphone, tablet or computer. If you are using responsive text it is not necessary you have to make extra efforts to increase the value of the messages and you're secure.

5. Break up the text

One thing that greatly diminish the impact of messages is using too lengthy paragraphs, as well as lacking breaks.

Avoid these two errors at all costs And, most important be sure that there aren't any hyperlinks that are too crowded in the same location. The key is getting straight to the point , and avoid situations where you're wandering around without any direction.

Automation of Your Email Campaign

Email marketing involves the sending of hundreds, if not thousands in emails sent to customers as well as others who might be interested in the data. So, it's normal for marketers to use online and other technical tools to run their campaigns and simplify their work. This is the point where email marketing can help.

Email automation is the use of software and other online methods to design and distribute information to a group of people at once. Thus, you just need to develop your marketing material choose a list of people and then use different tools to share them. The past was when newsletters had to be delivered via mail, and it required an extended time to record the addresses of each subscriber and send them these emails. Today, technology has assisted in easing the majority of these procedures, with automation becoming one of the most important methods. If you're not sure what to do to begin the automation process, you can follow the steps below for easy steps and instructions:

1. Develop an Viable Plan

The initial step to the development of a plan to achieve success is the development of a plan, which is also called a blueprint. This is where you must try to determine the kind of information you possess and your strategy of effectively integrating customer actions to the appropriate emails. There are some processes need to be customized and others that are more general. For example, some email messages that you can easily automate include:

* Welcome and introductory emails once a person has been signed up
* confirmation emails once you have completed specific actions like registering

* welcoming subscribers following an extended period of inactivity
* renewal reminders

General notification emails, e.g., notifying subscribers of a change in management of the company.

Be aware that the fact that these kinds of emails do not require segmentation does not mean they shouldn't be sent out in plain. Utilize a tool that can recognize the names of subscribers, and make sure that they are listed on the header of your email. For instance, "Welcome aboard, Beth we appreciate your subscribership." When you have an appropriate plan and you're ready to move onto the next stage.

2. The Best Method of Automation

When you've got your strategy completed, you need to pick the automated method which will work for your needs best. In general there are three email service levels that include freemium, mid-tier, as well as enterprise models. Based on the type of email that you're sending pick one of these options depending on your needs and budget.

* A freemium automation program offers a variety of free software that provides basic functions with the possibility of improvements in the near future. These tools are great for those who are new to marketing and aren't yet getting knack of the method of email marketing as it can be a huge help in educating novice users as well as getting them ready for the usage of more advanced tools. It is recommended to stay away from using this service except in a position where there is no money for additional tools, or you're working with an enterprise that doesn't really require advanced tools, and your subscriber base is growing at a remarkably tiny pace.

* The mid-tier tools for campaigns is more advanced and essential when you want to create an outstanding campaign. There are a myriad of additional features in this tool and it is geared on enhancing functionality even as you expand. The users who can benefit from this tool are those who are growing or mid-market companies, businesses that want to significantly increase the number of email addresses

they have, as well as experienced marketers. If you've got key performance indicators you want to attain and having goals clearly defined then this could be the best option for you.

* Lastly, you can make use of enterprise-based tools that provide a variety of advantages all in one. If you choose to utilize this tool, bear in mind that this tool is specifically designed for the most sophisticated of marketers, which implies that it's mostly utilized by professionals. The individuals who are best at using this tool are large corporations with an in-house email team or companies that demand the highest quality of customized services, and companies where the number of emails that must be sent out is at least a thousand.

There is no limitation to the kind of device you're obliged to utilize. But, you must evaluate your company and seek out professional guidance so that you can make the best option.

3. Configuring Your Workflow

This is the most straightforward aspect of the procedure. In this stage, you already have a tool for marketing to use and diverse content you would like to share with different subscribers. Thus, all you have to do is connect the particular automated messages to the subscribers of the particular category you would like to target. A good example of a tool that contains subscriber's commands is the following:

Figure 5. A diagram of an automatization tool using the ability to send marketing emails.

As can be seen from the image in the figure, the email marketing company has already categorizes existing and prospective subscribers into four groups.

Depending on the category into which the subscribers are, a particular message is delivered to them. For example, there's an automated message sent to those who are new to the service likely consisting of welcome messages, emails that are based on dates that are accrued to subscribers, and general emails that are sent out to all subscribers whenever modifications occur. Your workflow must be customized to your particular requirements and you should not replicate the processes of other individuals.

4. Reviewing and testing

The final stage of automation. It is the study of comprehensive information that will show how users are engaging and responding in your messages. The majority of automation tools come with analytical capabilities for data that allow them to determine the precise outcomes of certain events like users who have liked, who opened emails, and clicks. Utilize these data to improve your work by analyzing the emails that generated the highest number of hits, and ones that had the lowest. Once you've got an understanding of what's going on improving and refining your strategies becomes more straightforward.

Chapter 6: How To Keep Messages Out Of The Spam Folder

The spam folder may also be known as junk folder, or junk mailbox. It is a storage space for unwanted emails , as identified by the spam filters. The spam folders are filled with emails that are filtered either by the mailserver or user-friendly email program, and consider to be unwelcome. Most often, spam emails are composed of a number of messages with similar content that are sent to multiple recipients, as well as email filtering is generally capable of identifying these emails from servers and block them. If an email is flagged as spam There are a variety of disadvantages that can be incurred by the company that sent the email and include:

* The messages that portray negative images of the company

* many non-responsive recipients

There is a lot of money and time being wastage by the department of marketing that has no benefit.

If you are an email marketing expert If you are an email marketer, you may find yourself sending several messages that have the same content, to your email list. According to the article, mail servers could flag these emails as being spamming, limiting your efforts to get your message to as many people as you want to. To make sure that your messages do not get buried in a spam box There are a range options you could use, which include:

Conforming to the requirements of the CAN-SPAM Requirements

The term CAN-SPAM refers to the Controlling the Assault on Non-Solicited Marketing and Pornography law that was adopted on the 13th of December 2013 by the Federal Trade Commission. The function of this law will be to control commercial messages in order to stop businesses from causing distress to potential customers with unwelcome messages. The CAN-SPAM Act includes bulk messages as well as commercial emails. When electronic mail is being sent for the intention of advertising products or services, or even for the purpose of delivering promotions to customers, the

CAN-SPAM rules are to be observed completely.

The law also covers business-to-business emails , except for relationships and transactional messages. Most of the time there are no limitations on the sending of emails by companies to customers who are already customers or people who have inquired about their products or services even if they do not have a choice to receive messages. For instance, if you're a member of the National Bank of X, they have the authority to send you emails whenever they feel appropriate. These messages are known as relationship-related messages, and you are able to send as many messages as you like.

The messages that are considered transactional, on contrary, are intended to communicate transactional information and facilitate or affirm the agreement of a transaction, or providing information to a customer about an ongoing process. For instance, in event that a buyer purchases an item from a website the receipt that is sent via the email is referred to as an transactional message.

As an email marketing professional, you must make sure that your emails comply with the three components of CAN-SPAM, if they're not transactional or relational. The three CAN-SPAM groups of rules are content compliance as well as unsubscribe content. sending behaviour.

Content Compliance

Email marketers are bound by the CANSPAM act to adhere to the principles of content in emails. The content has to be precise and pertinent to subjects in a manner that isn't in any way misleading. Additionally, the physical address of the advertiser or publisher has to be valid. In this instance postal box addresses are the most suitable. If an outside party is sending emails, the correct physical address for the company that is whose product or service is advertised by emails must be listed. For instance, if you hire an email marketing firm to conduct your campaign, be sure your address is clearly stated in the emails.

The right to unsubscribe

The CAN-SPAM Act requires every email to contain unsubscribing buttons, which allow recipients to opt-out from the list of email recipients. The opt-out button should not be ambiguous or obscure and must be simple and easy to find. The majority of professional email marketers point users to the unsubscribing option when they decide to opt-out of receiving emails. The general CAN-SPAM policy is that, if a customer chooses to unsubscribe, the sender has 10 days to cease sending emails to the recipient.

Two examples of businesses fully in compliance with the option to unsubscribe, such as the ease with which it is possible to unsubscribe

Questions? Visit the Help Center

Netflix International B.V.

Unsubscribe | Terms of Use | Privacy | Help Center

Figure 6. Illustration of the unsubscribe option offered by Netflix. [10]

> If you believe this has been sent to you in error, please safely unsubscribe.

Figure 7. Illustration for the opt-out feature from Jumia. [11]

It is clear that there is no confusion or issue in finding the opt-out option within the two emails. One is able to unsubscribe at any time they wish.

The Compliance of the Sending Behaviour

The mandatory behavior of sending is comprised of the rules that were outlined in the two previous guidelines. Additionally, the other sending practices required by CAN-SPAM could be summarized in the following manner:

Beware of using misleading or false header data. The header must contain the address of the sender and recipient of the message, as well as the name of the field that originated and the address of email. Each address must be correct and capable of identifying who is the representative of the business that initiated the email.

* If sending emails that are not solicited to a person, it should be clear that the message is a marketing or advertisement, especially when recipients have not signed up for the kind of messages. The law also says that the receiver is entitled to block businesses from sending them emails and may sue if businesses continue to send emails.

Avoid using false topic lines and clearly display the content of your message and the purpose that you are sending the mail.

* The message must be clearly identified as an advertisement when you're just sending out advertisements. The CAN-SPAM law has clearly defined laws that define the tactics that marketers who use email in ensuring that their purpose must be clearly visible and not hidden behind other kind of message.

A marketer who sends an email must provide the recipient with the address where they live. The email must be sent to an actual physical address that includes an official P.O Box address associated in the US Postal address. If it is private mailboxes the address must be registered with the address with the commercial mail agency that is part of the postal service.

A marketer for email must inform the recipient of how to unsubscribe from receiving emails. Unsubscribing options should be clearly and easily visible in the email, and should be at least at the end of an email. This is merely to remind the need to adhere to the unsubscribe principle.

• Monitor what other people do on behalf of you in particular if a company is advertising for you. You remain responsible for following the CAN-SPAM law and are accountable for all information that is that is sent on behalf of you. If you find something wrong you should take it care of immediately.

Please follow the opt-out instructions promptly. The request to opt-out is to be dealt with in a matter of minutes or within ten days. Unsubscribing options should be functional in the initial 30 days following sending.

If you know the fundamentals of the CANSPAM act and try to adhere to their guidelines to the letter it is likely that only a small percentage messages, if any, your messages will be filtered into the folder of spam.

The CAN-SPAM Act is applicable to both people who initiate and the senders of commercial emails. The initiators are the ones who are the ones who create the message emails or who hire third party companies to send these messages on behalf of them. As the initiator, you have to comply with the rules as stated above, with the exception of the opt-out option that is only applicable to the senders.

They are owners of the products and services that are advertised or promoted in commercial messages. They are the primary ones responsible for an opt-out request. their physical address needs to be mentioned in the emails that are sent.

It's evident that initiators and senders can be a bit unclear, as they could be linked. For clarity the case, if a firm is in the business of affiliate marketing, and it is sending commercials to promote products offered by a specific company in turn, both the affiliate as well as the company have the responsibility of initiating. However, the business itself is the sender and its email address is the only one needed in the email, and the option to unsubscribe. For the ease and security of the process All initiators and recipients must make sure that they're following the CAN-SPAM rules to the letter. Likewise, affiliate companies must refrain from engaging with companies that are unsatisfactory in a few of the fundamental principles due to two main reasons.

First of all, the fact that these emails lack certain components will make them unusable, and will be placed within the junk mail folder. This will waste your time and energy.

In addition the fact that you are responsible for the emails you send. In the event that you get in trouble, you will not be able to get out and are more likely to lose lots of money due to the settlement of settlements.

Best HTML Email Tips

HTML can be an abbreviation that means Hypertext Mark-up Language. So the term "HTML" refers to an HTML email is the method by which email template's and the web page's codes for text and images are integrated. HTML differs from conventional simple text-based image system. Typically, the plain text image refers to text that is regular, without setting options for modifying it, such as bold underline, italic or other layout options that are unique.

The majority of emails are read today on mobile devices This trend has grown dramatically. Some mobile users are picky and more than half of them close or remove messages that aren't properly optimized for mobile phones. The more recipients erase messages, the greater chance of them being branded as spam. The use of responsive HTML design for email allows the user to browse emails on mobile devices in an the most optimal way, resulting in their satisfaction and this is beneficial to email marketers. A few of the best HTML email templates include fluid layouts, the use of techniques for coding, such as images and media queries and customized versions to your mobile viewers.

Fluid layouts are an example of a web page design where the layout of the page changes size when windows' size modified. It also defines the portion of the page with using percentages rather than fixed dimensions of pixel widths. For instance, when you choose to use the autorotate feature the fluid layout will ensure that content is resized in accordance with.

Media queries are functions that allow the content on a website to adapt to various screen sizes and resolutions. There are a variety of devices that favor this format because it is easy and simple to utilize and suitable for serving diverse content. In general, the viewport's width as well as width is the two most commonly used questions used in these.

How HTML keeps messages from the Spam Folder

Utilizing HTML is among the best methods to prevent emails from being filtered into in the folder of spam. There are several guidelines you must be following to avoid messages becoming spam. They include:

Always send a properly formatted HTML email.

* Remove email with only images.

* Include at minimum two paragraphs of text with every graphic that is used within the message.

* Try your best to maximize the quality of your photos.

* Proper layout. On mobile screens some designs are difficult to scroll through and the single-column layout can be considered the best. This layout allows your email to be accessible to all devices, making it simple to read.

* Font. The font must be easily visible and simple to read. If the font you choose to use has a small size, the text can be

difficult to read and not many people would be willing to make their eyes strain to see the tiny text. In the end, these readers are more likely to simply ignore the email, without even reading it. As mentioned, always use font sizes 13 , 14 and 13 for your text, and in the case of titles, 22 pixels.

* Images. Mobile devices load images and web content much more slow than computers. Images are more hefty than text, and require more long to load. To ensure that readers are not lost and save bandwidth, make sure to make use of smaller and more responsive images. Mobile devices come with high resolution displays and require twice as big images than standard mobile images to ensure that users receive a high quality image.

* Buttons. Buttons allow readers to include text, especially when some or all of them are inclined to participate in an ongoing discussion. The buttons must be large enough to allow the users to be able to clearly see them, and entice them to

read your email. A size of 40x40 pixels is recommended, but greater if it is possible.

* Offers. It is crucial to put your most important products or the most valued deal above the text, since the majority of people who read the email won't look down to find the best offer or "buy immediately" button. Make sure you include the most important element of your message as there's not enough space to incorporate all of the information on the phone version. Limit the amount of products and offers available for the mobile version, if the email is usually full. The desktop version doesn't need to be compatible to the mobile device. Reduce the contents of your emails, as your targeted readers will be able to transition to better rates of translation.

* Test. The most crucial thing to take prior to sending emails to your customers is to ensure that the content is perfect. Make sure that your designs look flawless across all major kinds of smartphones. The most commonly used ways to test your HTML email are platforms like Litmus as well as

Email with Acid. But the best method to carry the tests on the actual device.

Benefits of HTML email compared to plain text emails

There are many advantages to making use of HTML message text instead of plain text emails. The advantages are:

An HTML text email isn't boring since the text is laid out in blocks, columns and sections to ensure that the user can quickly look through the text and quickly discover what they are looking for.

Images, animations and occasionally videos are sometimes included within HTML versions. Thus rich media is created and usually captures the attention of the readers.

Links that can be clicked are important in newsletters and are accessible with HTML versions. It is always possible to have a higher chance of someone taking the appeal to action if the emails' content is compelling enough. The more interactions with emails, the less probability of receiving spam.

Automation and marketing tools like "smart Content" can be utilized to speak directly to your subscribers. HTML-based emails can be the sole method to send highly customized emails when marketers of email want to send an individual email to every subscriber on the list.

People are more attracted by the latest trends. A beautiful layout, attractive colors for the eyes, contemporary graphics and multimedia will immediately draw the visitor to go to the site.

A HTML email newsletter can be made using templates which can be a major benefit for many and an advantage over text-only email.

When using HTML mail, it's possible to save the tracking code that aids in the improvement of the quality of content as well as other functions that are added in the following steps

You can include legal information as well as the option to unsubscribe inside the form of an HTML text newsletter. This is in compliance with the law by offering the reader the opportunity to opt out at any time they'd like.

While HTML email is more flexible and efficient than plain text emails however, there are certain situations in which an email marketer might choose to send a plain text message. Therefore, the majority of skilled marketers can combine both. Make sure you get all the information you can on the application of HTML in email marketing and you'll notice an impressive decrease in spam-related cases.

Utilizing Email Software

Email software is an add-on that can be useful when it comes to using electronic mail. They function as editors for emails using various formats, layouts and tools for messaging which allow emails to be personalized with different style of writing. Email software utilizes a variety of host services for email. A lot of users of email software use hosted email hosted by IPSs (Intrusion Prevention Systems) and others, while some set their email addresses, which could require an editor for emails or tools for editing emails.

There are a variety of email software applications , which include Microsoft Outlook, Windows Live Mail, Inbox by Gmail and Mozilla Thunderbird, Mailbird, Outlook Express and eM clients, Postbox, Bat and Front. Each one of them has innovative features to manage emails.

Other applications include open-source or freeware tools for sending and receiving email messages such as WYSIWYG editors to create emails, antispam and antiphishing security advanced search capabilities as well as rules and filters to improve effectiveness.

Microsoft Outlook

Microsoft Outlook is the most widely used software application. Many of the business email traffic that is generated by Windows and the Windows operating system are handled with Microsoft Outlook. As with any other software for email Outlook provides its transfer interface that has features like multiline display and various types of filtering and tools for folders.

Outlook calendar, email and contact management systems are functions that are connected to give users a lot of involvement.

eM Client

eM Client stands out as the most widely used email program that supports an extensive range of email providers and has the capability for chat integration, smart translation, and easy migration. Through eM client, it's simple to move your email from Gmail as well as iCloud and outlook.com by adding your email address which it will adjust to your personal preferences. Additionally, calendars and contacts are able to be imported with eM client and deleted if you wish to run them on your own. A chat application integrated into the interface is available within eM client, and can be used by platforms like Jabber or Google Chat. Its capabilities are far superior than the ones available within the Webmail user interface. In contrast to other free email applications, eM client is packed with advanced features including automated translation, delayed send encryption, and delayed send. As a result it is perfect to manage two email accounts. Upgrade to eM Client Pro if you have additional accounts, gain access to VIP support, or even for commercial use.

Thunderbird

The program is based on tabs that include chart and calendars. When an email is created the new window is opened completely. The majority of people use Thunderbird because it's an open source and comes with a variety of features , such as being able to browse on the web in a correct manner. Furthermore, Thunderbird integrates Google Chat, IRC, Twitter, and XMPP so that apps are able to be used within Thunderbird and without requiring migration.

Mailbird

Mailbird is missing labels and text in the pages. Instead, they're substituted by icons. Mailbird can be integrated with around 50 apps , such as Trello, Slack, Asana as well as chat tools like WhatsApp as well as WeChat. It is therefore an important communication platform.

Windows Mail

This is a standard app that is included with Windows. On the left-hand side in Windows Mail, one can access your calendar, tasks and your inbox. The options for snoozing, possibility to schedule messages or HTML editing aren't available on Windows Mail. However, there's an option to draw in Word.

Postbox

While email templates can save many hours of work, Postbox improves models by making it possible to tailor templates to the individual who is receiving. Postbox has a built-in editor that utilizes placeholders to give easily automated numbers to field names, dates or any other piece of information that is stored in the email that was received or in the Postbox itself. Postbox also has features like an HTML editor that forms part of the composition windows and works with popular management tools like OneDrive as well as Dropbox.

Bat

The Bat app is made to safeguard and address security concerns that aren't common however they could affect the other emails sent to users. Bat is equipped with a key that can unlock all the data that is stored; therefore it is able to be accessed through the application it self, and not from other clients that allow the information can be accessed from outside the application. Data that is managed using fly disk encryption provides additional security to the backup system that is effective. Bat is highly regarded by people due to its use of end-to end encryption that not only protects information, particularly sensitive data, but is also the only one to connect several email accounts.

Front

Front was created to enable teams to collaborate within shared mailboxes. In default, all mailboxes that are created are private. It is possible to allow certain team members to access certain mailboxes, and then assign an email to them from in the emails. Front also offers chat features.

Thus, you are able to get connected with other team members through the application. Front also includes an analytical section which is focused on issues that concern customers with emails that have been sent, because it's an application for businesses.

Software for email and junk mail

Spam emails can be diminished by ensuring they do not get into the inbox or other important folders through the use of antispam software or the use of web security. While it's not simple to stay clear of spam emails however, they can be eliminated or reduced through the making use of antispam programs. The majority of spam filters can discern legitimate messages from messages that aren't without much user involvement. If a spam message is not detected in the process of filtering, messages could be detected as spam by users, which allows the filters to adjust to new threats. There is also more sophisticated software that can provide phishing security which is usually used when emails appear authentic, but isn't.

Therefore, phishing security is a must in any antispam software.

A good spam program should be included in conjunction with an antivirus program as most of these spam messages contain malware and viruses. Security for your computer is made easy with one software suite which assures the system's reliability. Although it is a common practice to divert messages from inboxes as well as other important folders for emails ensure that you have an antivirus software to ensure that your computer is not infected in the event that you open an unintentionally spam email.

Check and the Cap Email Frequency

Frequency is the maximum amount of messages an individual contact may receive within the specified time, whether it is weekly or monthly or annual. When the maximum number has been attained and no further messages are sent to the person in question, email frequency is considered to have been limitless.

Frequency capping is the primary feature that is found in every marketing automation platform. It permits email marketers to communicate information to all contacts in the database, and without the worry of infringing upon the privacy of those recipients. This feature allows the business to safeguard its reputation by not being rejected through the sending of a lot of messages to the user at all times. Thus, messages from the company will not be branded as spam.

The email frequency limits can be set to stop sending too often messages to contacts. You can also set the maximum number of emails which can be sent out to contacts in the course of a certain time. This is especially important in the case of sending automated messages. This is due to the fact that you no have to be concerned about sending automated messages, as well as other marketing initiatives that are overwhelming to your contacts. This can result in what's known as "contact fatigue" in marketing via email. The setting up of an email frequency protection

An ideal email practice is to keep your subscribers interested and not overflowing their inboxes. Frequency safeguards can establish the maximum number of marketing emails a contact can receive over a specific time. The emails that transition from one email to another sent via CRM (CRM) do not form included in the frequency cap , and will be sent to recipients. Transactional emails don't increase the frequency after the limit has been reachedand is not part of the limit of frequency. Even though you set a frequency limit it's difficult to monitor all messages that are sent to every individual. As an email marketing professional, it is important to avoid sending excessive emails to your subscribers since your relationship with prospects or customer is vital to keep.

Best email practices for email marketing frequency

To achieve a balance in marketing via email, the email marketer must be following the best practices in email marketing. There are three methods that provide the best results when it comes to determining marketing frequency , which includes:

Users can choose the frequency

Give users the chance to select the frequency of emails they'd like. This is essential because the user won't complain that they don't receive the email they signed up to receive or be getting too many emails that aren't relevant. In addition to a variety of personalization options feeds also permit users to choose how often they want to receive the email.

Relevant content

The email marketing professional should be responsible for the content of emails. The email marketer should focus on quality and not quantity. Be careful with the the content and it should avoid being misleading and insignificant. Images and graphics are encouraged to grab the attention of the reader. Promotional and informational emails must be mixed to make the content appealing educational, informative, and promotional and attracts the reader's attention. The recipient will not be upset by the frequency of email when the messages are relevant. They will open , read and click on the emails to their mailbox. Many subscribers opt-in to receive emails to be given a gift. Therefore, it is recommended to include gifts in your email campaign.

Test the test, then modify, and then try Test, adjust, and test

There is a way to determine what your customers want from their email messages by asking them for comments on what they love or don't like. The most dangerous thing you could be doing as an email marketing professional is follow the other businesses blindly since they all have distinct audience offerings and objectives. It is crucial to continually conduct A/B tests to see if you can improve to be able to improve in the future. Always do a test until you are confident that you have what is required in your email. The best approach is to listen to the requirements of your people you are communicating with and do all you can to satisfy the expectations of your audience.

Limitation on setting frequency limits for email caps

The setting of frequency may take more time than you expect when making bulk deliveries to send. When preparing delivery the evaluation of contacts is carried out to determine if they are in compliance with the frequency cap of their email account settings, this can be carried out in a separate manner. If the delivery contains many contacts and you've set up multiple limits on frequency, this can take more time than you anticipated to prepare the delivery for deliver. When you set the frequency cap for email be sure to take into consideration the need to prevent the possibility of causing fatigue to your customers when you send large quantities of deliveries. Contact fatigue is the condition in which customers are exhausted getting emails. They may end up not responding the email, deleting it, unsubscribing or even sending an email in the junk mailer.

What causes email fatigue?

Email fatigue can be the result of either sending out content that is not relevant to the user or sending emails to frequently. Be sure to avoid email fatigue by sending less emails. If you send the wrong message to an address that you didn't intend to send to can cause them to become bored of receiving your messages.

The effects of fatigued email can sabotage your marketing campaign, particularly when emails aren't tailored to the recipients or triggered by a specific user behaviour. The whole database will become tired when this happens, and in the event of it happening it is likely that many people will decide to opt out or mark the email as spam. Announcing an email as spam has a huge impact on revenues, especially when more emails are found by spam filtering.

A Consumer's Definition of Spam

Spam refers to bulk, unsolicited emails . It means that the receiver hasn't consented to the email marketing company in sending them an email. Bulk is a term used to describe a large quantity of messages that contain nearly the same contents. There's been an improvement in the past since messages began to go directly to the spam folders. Recently, the public has changed the meaning of spam, and the word is used even for emails that appear legitimate. Certain consumers might refer to emails as spam even when they are aware of the sender. They might flag messages to the spam folder, even though they've opted into the message. Certain individuals may sign into your emails but continue to forward messages in the junk folder. When lots of people get a flood of messages that aren't relevant or irrelevant, they flag the message as spam. Many promotional messages are thus, more likely to be considered spam. Notifying recipients may not be enough to protect the message from being flagged as spam.

The meaning of spam has led to difficulties over the years. If an unwanted bulk email could constitute an advertisement a scam or even a simple message whose content is insignificant and is delivered unpackaged, the message is described in the context of "spam." A lot of legislators have wasted much of their time trying to regulate the content of spammessages, trying to address various issues, but not being aware that the problem arises from the distribution of emails.

Technically speaking, spam can be described as an email message which is not relevant and does not have a personal identity and the sender is not knowingly consenting to the email being delivered. Numerous authorities have been used to determine what constitutes to as spam, with an example of this is the CAN-SPAM Act from 2004. The law offers a unique method of dealing with spam and, as a result there are different definitions of what is considered to be spam and what is considered a spam.

According to Spamhaus the bulk email that is not sent out to users does not concern content but consent as per the definition of industrial standard. Thus, debates regarding whether spam falls under the

CAN-SPAM act or is in compliance with the CANSPAM act are irrelevant.

Information about bulk email spam

Unsolicited bulk email messages are not permitted from being distributed by ISPs. (ISPs).

Spamhaus' antispam block list, known as the SBL is used by a large number of internet users. Worldwide spam is known as bulk unsolicited email (UBE). If you send UBE online regardless of whether the message is commercial or unlawfully sent, the person who is the sender of the message is automatically considered a spammer. Spammers could lose their Internet account or be banned from the Spamhaus Block List (SBL) when they send messages that are spam, since they're breaking the law. The perception of consumers about spam have changed dramatically and has led to an equally significant change in email marketing strategies. Litmus and Fluent conducted a study of over 1,300 Americans by using Fluent technology to discover the meaning of spam to consumers. The study concluded that people will opt out of receiving emails and mark emails as spam based on the same reasons mentioned earlier. Consumers can also experience experiences that go beyond their inbox. Through incorporating these changes marketers can prevent the issue of spam and build customer relationships.

Extension of customer relations

ISPs and marketers for email should strive to prevent complaints from customers and extend their relationship. This is possible by making sure that your consent to email strategy is effective. The consent to email must be sought and in the appropriate frequency. Always design mobile-friendly emails as well as an easy web page. Allow for easy opt-outs so that customers don't have to be frustrated when they might wish to unsubscribe. Don't contact clients after having a an unpleasant experience with your company and make sure you always respect your clients' preferences.

ISPs are required by law to make sure their customers are happy. ISPs and email marketers are seeking solutions to manage the industry and differentiate between email marketing and spam.

Reputation and verification

ISPs decide if emails originate from the domain they attribute to. Certain companies evaluate on the credibility of either the provider or outgoing domains according to their email practices as well as complaints about spam. Certain IPSs employ this guideline to put certain email providers on a whitelist, which allows images and links to pass through the spam filter.

Third certified by a third party

Websites are accountable to protect the privacy of consumers. Certain businesses have gone to the point of certifying customers as legitimate. They assure that the sender is compliant with the accepted practices. IPSs permit the messages of a reliable sender to be delivered directly into inboxes.

Certification debate

There have been debates regarding how to limit the spam emails. Some legislators believe that email marketers should be paid per email that they send out to check for unresponsive email addresses which would limit the amount of emails that are delivered to people who do not require these messages. Many marketers are not in favor of the notion of paying per email, given that the commercial marketing budget could be increased by a third. While some marketers may be able to pay for the expense, many aren't. Some, like nonprofits and content producers can't afford it even if they could.

Be mindful of the customer

While third party certification places the burden on the consumer's consent however, there's an important reason to ensure that consumers are satisfied in the event that the third party does not change the focus on consent from consumers.

The removal of spam from email marketing will only increase the cost after setting up additional security settings and creating spam filters. The bottom line is that ensuring the customer's permission is the best method to ensure that email messages contain useful links and images in the subscribers' inbox. This is possible by whitelisting, inclusion or third-party verification.

Testing Spam Risks

A spam test checks emails to determine if certain filters for spam will block the email from the inbox of subscribers. The test examines the contents of the email as well as the domain used to send the email. The inability to handle spam poses problems like wasting hours trying to find legitimate messages that have been lost in mailer, or the mailbox being overloaded with messages and, in the case of an organization, the costs that spammers incur is extremely large, in terms bandwidth and storage on hard drives.

There are numerous tools available to determine if your email has a chance being branded spam. The tools you can use include

An email with an Acid tool

If you are using Email with Acid as a test tool, then you could conduct a spam test with the seed list and, in this the test is sent through an SMTP server or the test is run through the server. A test using a seed list provides more precise results. This is because the test thoroughly for various aspects of the mailer that may be considered spam. The test does not just look at subject lines and contents but also look at the IP address or domain to determine if it is blocked.

Spam testing using seed list test

A seed list test typically gives exact results when you use the Email Service Provider (ESP). Seed lists have an internal email address that tests emails are sent out to. This includes family members, coworkers members, or family members. An email address is necessary to be able to use a variety of clients. It is possible to determine whether the email passes through the various spam filters for email.

If you're making use of email on acid, or the Email on Acid platform, you can find a seed list in the spam testing section. The list of email addresses in the ESP is copied and pasted into the test for spam prior to creating the test emails. The list changes over time , as one tests the test again. To ensure exact results you must duplicate and copy the email from your test directly into the list of seeders.

The testing of spam with Litmus

The majority of your time could be spent creating an appropriate email. But, despite the efforts and time put into it some of these emails may end being tossed into the trash folder, rather than within the inbox. This could happen without even noticing. Litmus analyzes the email for numerous blacklists and tests. Litmus detects any issues that could hinder you from receiving emails and offers a plan to correct the issue. Spam testing is crucial because it allows email to get into your inbox.

Test of the spam filter and inbox

Tests of spam filters and Inbox are paid services that typically offered through Email on Acid. Inbox test lets you look at campaigns that are run by various email clients, while the test for filtering allows you to test whether a your campaign fails or passes certain spam filters.

Glockapp spam tool

Glockapp distinguishes between spam and inbox location, providing the user with complete and accurate information about the inbox. This spam tool checks the authenticity of senders and checks email against spam filtering. It also compares your email address to blacklists.

Mailtrap

This kind of tool can perform a comprehensive testing of emails that can be done using email. It is possible to test HTML to make sure it is compatible using the client for email. The entire test is conducted on a fake server which means that there's no way to accidentally send an email test to your users.

Check out my Email

This tool was created to examine the codes of different email platforms and clients. It's unique in that it provides multiple options to check your email. The tool allows you to upload your files directly or copy and paste the content of your emails and then email to a particular preview your Email inbox.

Inbox Inspector

Inbox Inspector lets you look at emails in more than 25 of the most popular email clients, including the most prominent desktop and webmail clients and mobile-based email applications.

HTML Email Checker

This tool is free to authenticate the mark-up like HTML, XHTML, or CSS, of newsletters and emails. It also examines the authenticity of links, images, and tests for accessibility.

Mail Tester

This can be used to examine the emails for red flags that indicate spam. It looks at emails and important words that signify spam to algorithms, as well as other indicators. Mail Tester allows users to determine if they are blocked by major email programs.

Sender Score

Sender Score examines the credibility of the sender by entering their domain name and IP address to get the report on how trustworthy the person you're putting your trust in as recipient of emails.

Postmarks

This can be used to avoid the need to wish to send an email to a test link. It's a simple instrument for obtaining scores as well as improving the quality of your emails. Email codes are cut and pasted in a simple-to-use interface that is simple to use to examine different types of email to determine the spam score.

Reputation Authority

If you are looking to evaluate the quality and quantity of emails you've written, Reputation Authority is used. The tool utilizes a domain that process the reputation that an individual has earned over time. The report includes historical data that allows you to determine whether you're reliable by looking up the domain or if you're facing coming issues.

The importance of testing for spam

Spam testing is essential due to:

* It allows you to determine if you are on the blacklist.

It also makes sure the infrastructure you have setup to be successful. Email validation is carried out correctly to ensure that your record is correctly set up.

* You can receive advice on how to improve the quality of your emails to enhance the effectiveness of your email campaign. This is done through troubleshooting assistance available.

* Messages are pre-screened across the main spam filters, including webmail and inbox providers, as well as score-based filtering is also integrated to filter spam.

Chapter 7: How To Create Relevant Messaging Using Effective Subject Lines And Smart Designs

Making relevant emails for marketing purposes requires more than simply putting a sequence of sentences and then presenting them as final content. After you've created the email and refined every sentence, the actual work is to begin. It is possible that you are in a position that you've racked your head for hours and come an idea for an idea that is the best of subject phrases. However, the actual analysis of the effectiveness of the work you've done is when you examine the stats and figure out the extent of clicks and openings that are in line with your expectations. Naturally, when the end result is not in line with what you expected, the result is a higher level of discontent, which can be quite sad. As we learned in the previous part One of the reasons that cause the low numbers is that content doesn't meet the expectations of its readers. How do you ensure that the content created meets the standards set by the public and also meets the purpose of the concept?

The Art of Writing Subject Lines that are Perfect Subject Line

The best methods by which you can ensure that you create the best message for your email is by nailing the topic line. We've previously discussed the importance of having a flawless headline, but I'll be sure to reiterate this point by stating that your subject line will the first step to your marketing email campaign. So, a weak subject line is bound to cause failure, whereas the best line will not only guarantee that recipients will open emails but also affect the extent that they will take the email seriously. There are several techniques you can apply to write a great copy, among them:

1. Use Language that is Effective

The usage of actionable language doesn't just mean using words but it has been proved to be a psychological influence which aids. Imagine receiving an email with a subject line that includes "prepare your accounting statement in 1 hour." If you receive such an email there's no confusion or ambiguity as to what exactly the email is about. Be aware that the language used in actionable is simple, and it will clearly state what needs to be completed. The above message triggers an entirely different reaction when compared to a similar message with the subject line "Will you be able to prepare your accounting reports in one hour in the second instance, this is a query that is not specific, which means that the person could strive to meet the demands of the email, or not. If you ask someone to perform something within a specified period of time, you're giving them the green light to refuse and to negotiate. With the use of actionable language, there is no other option and the person must do what is requested.

In some cases you may be able to twist actionable language. This means that you won't only relying on verbs, but you will have the freedom and ability to play with the language insofar as the message is simple. Actionable language doesn't mean that you are directing someone to do things, and it is important to be aware of this. For instance, a sentence that reads, "Do not miss the largest concert that you can find in the United States," is an actionable phrase, and is not a demand in the slightest. The marketing person doesn't tell you that it's essential to purchase tickets for the concert, but instead encourages you to do so gently. And once you've been convinced you are, there is a good probability of you heeding the appeal to act.

2. Make sure that clarity is more important than the desire for a catchy sound.

If you are sending out an email to promote your business It is obvious that your main goal could be to make your email appealing in order to grab the attention of your readers and increase the chances of subscribing to or listening to your emails. Although there is no doubt that the importance of being catchy but it is important to note that clarity is of greater significance. When it comes to email marketing, do not compromise on clarity in the name of entertaining. Although people love jokes and puns but it's of no benefit to entertain them and fail to get any action from them as they aren't aware of the purpose of your email.

3. Personalization

We've already talked about the importance of personalizing subjects in our previous section, but I feel forced to remind you of how crucial this is. There are plenty of emails that are sent out by bots in the modern world and I am able to tell that the people you contact are looking for customized messages that are designed specifically for their needs. As we've discussed previously, among the best methods to create personalization is to add the name of the initial email recipient on your subject line.

4. No Clickbait

If you find that receiving unfeeling messages from bots makes you feel uneasy it is likely that using clickbait can be even more disturbing. It is true that your goal might be to convince people to read your emails but it's essential to ensure that you're performing this in a proper method. The content of the subject line must be exactly the same as what is in the body of the email and there's no question regarding this. If you are a regular user of clickbait users are accustomed to it and it's an absolute turn-off. In the end, people lose faith in you, so your emails won't be opened.

5. Beware of shouting

There are numerous ways to write that scream spam One of them is the overuse of caps and exclamation marks when writing the subject. Think about the subject line:

If such an email lands in your inbox, one of the primary things the capitalized letters as well as the heightened exclamation points accomplish is to increase your awareness. You might think that using such a technique will draw your attention however the reality is that it is successful in bringing you to be the type that is negative. The majority of people are comfortable with being bombarded with spam today that they'll never bother opening and seeing something that screams spam. The frequent punctuation can scream spam and you'll most certainly end up on the spam lists of most of your clients.

6. Utilize Psychology to your Advantage

Humans are extremely competitive by nature This can cause them to want to always staying on top of the game and that means the average person is unlikely to be satisfied when not enjoying something others seem to be enjoying. When you write your topic lines be sure to keep these psychology tips in mind. Then discover a method of working with them to ensure you are getting the best results from your campaign.

Human beings don't like to be left out of any kind of thing. This is known in the form of fear of not being able to enjoy (FOMO). When using this tactic be sure to make it clear that you are in a hurry by making the recipients feel that if don't take the action call seriously, they'll be missing out on lots. For example, offer discount coupons and discounts that are timed or limit the number. Subject lines that follow this approach include:

<50% discount for the first 10 people who will purchase this LG system>

By using subject lines that are a bit more shrewd those who receive emails are aware that a lack of action could cost them the offer and are therefore more motivated to take action quickly. A lot of companies employ this method to increase sales and this technique generally works every time.

It is more probable for someone draw attention to your if they know that other people are also drawn to you. Although this could seem unfair and selfish however, that's just the way it is. The reason companies employ celebrities to promote their products is because of their influence. In the same way, people are likely to be more attentive to a person who has a significant impact on the lives of others. If I hold an entrepreneurial seminar while Mark Zuckerberg does the same at the same cost location, time, and even makes similar arguments individuals will naturally decide to listen to Zuckerberg instead. Consider that one way that you can influence readers through this strategy is to increase your social media presence and to ensure you have enough social proof that gives people the impression that you're great. The higher the level of social proof is, the more people will be more likely to read your emails.

Images also are a major factor in influencing the mental state of an individual. If someone is looking at a sad-looking face and is able to see it, they instantly be in a sad mood, as for other moods. Try to make use of images to communicate instantly the mood of the person and you'll be able to establish a more connections to your recipients of emails.

The art of writing the Perfect Email

If you're certain you've come up with an outstanding subject line, it's now time to concentrate on the design of an ideal email with the pertinent content. It is important to note that the way you design words, phrases, and the content will determine whether you are successful in grabbing the attention of your recipients and placing them at the top of the list for paying attention to the call to take action. The key points that will help you create the best email marketing material include:

1. Establishing Relevance

Relevance is still one of the most important elements of marketing via email regardless of whether you're merely writing the subject line or creating the entire content for the mailer. It is important to note that effective marketing via email isn't a matter by how well grammar is or proficiency in a specific language. What is important is the way you convey the message without being boring or obvious. While you're at making sure that you're still able to convey the message and don't diverge from the topic of the email. Take a look at the email below.

Figure 8. Illustration of an appropriate short email sent by Warby Parker Marketers.

From the moment you start your email message, its primary message or purpose is instantly apparent. They have utilized the power of images along with a concise and appealing color scheme to draw your attention and convey the message with the smallest words they can. When you first look at the advertisement you'll see an inscription on the front of the page that is placed in a larger size than the other words. It is sure to enthral your curiosity, and you'll want to know why the date has nothing to do with have to do with any aspect of. In this instance the prescription will expire on the day that it is due to expire and that is the primary reason for the email. The marketing team has not included any additional jargon or commentary, which demonstrates the significance of the message.

It is likely that the email didn't immediately inform you that your prescription is due to expire but instead, they wrote long paragraphs on the importance of glasses that are new, as well as advertising the latest glasses are on the market. This would be boring and unnecessary since you already understand the significance to wearing glasses (which is the reason you're wearing glasses in the first beginning).

2. The Second Person Writing

When you write emails for marketing purposes the goal should focus on writing in a way that makes readers feel as though you've written only to them. The second person writing style serves this goal, and you can make the recipients of your mail feel more personal while also giving them the impression of speaking to them. Some of the words that can help you write with the person of the other in a way that is sufficient are the use of pronouns like "you" or "your." Think about this two sentence:

For the very first phrase the writer has used Pronouns using the third person making the reader connect with the content being written. This contrasts to the second sentence, which follows an approach that is more general. Always try to target your email at the reader and not the general population.

3. Always identify the person you Send the message to

Knowing who you're aiming at is crucial. This is so crucial that it is mentioned in nearly every chapter we've looked at. Experts in email marketing claim that they prefer not to speak at all, rather than remain uninformed and unclear about the particular categories of people they're seeking to target. In a study that was conducted by UHURU regarding the reactions of consumers to certain emails marketing messages, they discovered that: Seventy-four percent of all users were extremely dissatisfied with web-based content they consider to be general and is also referred to as Infosys. These kinds of messages appear to be being sent out randomly and are not targeted at any particular person.

63% of customers were extremely upset when they received messages that were related to advertisements and were of a general appeal. The effect is even more severe when you're bombarded with messages that are not relevant to you even though you have not done anything to show that you're keen to receive such messages.

* More than 80% of respondents said that they felt more connected when the various brands and content marketing companies provided information that appeared to be individual, which made them feel appreciated.

Although we've talked about ways you can make your email recipients feel valued, the actual issue is the methods you can truly distinguish between people. Some of the most reliable ways to identify people include:

1. Find their own individual sources of suffering. Each need or desire humans strive to satisfy stems from gaps. You can't value something only if it actually helps you. That's why it's important for marketers of email to work hard and try to find out what people actually need. There is no way you can convince a person that a certain service or product is good for

them, if you do not know why they would need such a product/service/content. A few of the questions you can be asking yourself to gain more insight into the customers are:

What are the issues that email recipients could face? If, for instance, you're addressing people from one particular country only then you stand a better chance of pinpointing some of the biggest issues that people in the country are known to have to deal with. One example is when you are addressing people living in a nation with the highest rate of unemployment.

Sending emails , such as seems appropriate, considering that a majority of people might have had difficulty finding work at one point or one time or the other. The message your email campaign is supposed to convey is your knowledge of an issue, and the various ways you've got ideas to the most likely solution.

2. Get the readers hooked with an engaging headline. The significance of a relevant headline is emphasized. We've

already covered the topic of headlines thoroughly and the only thing I can suggest is to make sure that the subject is connected to the subject matter you are planning to discuss within the section on content.

3. Offer solutions. The initial step we talked about was trying to pinpoint the issues or pain points that recipients of mail have. After you've identified these issues, your task is to offer solutions. Make sure that the solutions you propose aren't just obvious but have a lot of advantages. Always remember it is your sole opportunity you need to prove your proficiency and demonstrate to your email recipients that you actually receive the message.

The very first and best aspect you must show genuine concern in your email marketing, and you can accomplish this by starting your email marketing with a respectful comment like follows:

"We recognize that finding a job is among the most difficult tasks you've ever had to tackle ...."

Conclusion

If it's properly executed If it is properly implemented, there are very few items that can equal the efficacy of an email marketing campaign.

Your small business must employ these methods to connect with your customers, in conjunction with organic SEO strategies and other traditional methods of advertising.

Contacting your customers via their emails is a great method to keep them updated and interested in your company. It's also one of the most cost-effective marketing strategies currently available.

If you follow the necessary measures to make sure that the messages aren't viewed as spam both by the inbox of your customer and the customers themselves, you'll be successful with this kind of marketing.

The most difficult aspect of an e-mail marketing campaign is to determine the appropriate frequency and amount of messages. Once you've found the "sweet spot" in your marketing, you'll be in all the time with your clients.

If your company isn't using an e-mail marketing method and you're losing out on a huge amount of money and customers' interest!

Thank you to download this book!

I hope that this book has been useful to determine the direction you'd prefer to go in.

www.ingramcontent.com/pod-product-compliance
Lightning Source LLC
Chambersburg PA
CBHW071836080526
44589CB00012B/1019